WILLIAM BO

Camera Obscura

Preface by
NOEL COWARD

London
WILLIAM   HEINEMANN   LTD,

MANUFACTURED IN THE UNITED STATES OF AMERICA

Grateful acknowledgment is hereby made to the New York World for permission to republish some of these essays in book form.

Contents

Contents

Preface

WILLIAM BOLITHO *died on the 2nd of June in Avignon, at the age of thirty-nine, leaving apart from his published books ("Leviathan," "Cancer of Empire," "Murder for Profit," "Italy under Mussolini," and "Twelve Against the Gods") a practically completed play, which he was revising finally when he was taken ill, and a large number of essays and articles, some of them unpublished, and the rest printed in the New York* World *and other papers. A selection from these is contained in this volume, and it is planned to publish those which have been omitted at a later date.*

This is an era of journalism, an odd phase in the history of civilisation, when the performances of the great and the small alike are distorted and over-coloured for the masses by a welter of journalistic clichés. Every human achievement, whether in science, music, painting, literature, or courageous endurance, is immediately torn down and denuded of its intrinsic beauty, and presented to the world, levelled and vitiated, through the medium of the newspapers. Surprisingly, William Bolitho stood in the midst of this dull confusion, the quality of his mind cutting through it like wire through a wedge of cheese. Not just once

1

Preface

in a way, which would have been easier, but regularly, three times a week for so many months in the year. It is good that we should view our times through the mind of a Poet, and in these strange years William Bolitho can open our eyes to happenings which we are in danger of accepting without seeing, and we should be deeply grateful to him.

I feel that the phrase, "the mind of a Poet," may need, perhaps, a slight explanation.

The mind of a Poet, as I see it, is a mind that colours life with imagination based on necessarily bitter experience, a mind that has survived the squalor of small humiliations and the melancholy of great disillusions, and remains unerring in the perception of beauty in the human heart. In all the essays in this book, even those in which the import is mainly satirical, this poetic tenderness persists, a quality of grace untainted by sentimentality, a gesture of recognition towards undying essentials, which most of us have too little time and too much self-consciousness to realise. This gesture, I believe, is in no way deliberate on William Bolitho's part, but entirely instinctive. He can illumine the tinselled sordidness of Montmartre, not from any conscious desire to do so, but because his mind is so constituted that it must invariably unearth intrinsic values even in absurdities. He writes of a cabaret, which in three short years has fallen from fashion, as having "an indefinable air of antiquity, not the precious aroma of centuries, but the shabby, premature aging of a clown." He writes of the supremely successful cabarets of the moment: "Fat carpets, saxophone bands, smooth floors, plush seats against the wall, are their unchanging regalia. Each has its gallery of business-like beauties, nonchalantly waiting for someone to pay their dinner. The range of material pleasures is limited. Man's brains have transformed the earth and the sea, but sensuality remains where it was before the flood. . . . The management sells children's toys, coloured celluloid balls to throw, and blue and red paper streamers, with paper caps, dolls, and the usual amusements of an infant birthday party. The man who has come a thousand miles for this is contented. For the glorious champagne that seems to freeze in the glass as the foam subsides is a famous trickster. Not only for the quick, certain profit do the managers of Montmartre insist on this wine alone being served. Without it, the sum of the world's pleasures might appear a little thin."

This particular form of description must bewilder those who persist in labelling writers either as romantic or realistic, because here, as in life itself, the two are inextricably mixed. There is poetry here, and satire, and a human understanding beyond tolerance.

As an excellent example of that quality, which is so often airily classified as "versatility," but which, being the complete adjustment of the writer's mind to the subject upon which he is engaged, is in reality the essence of true Art, I should like to refer the reader to an essay in this volume entitled "Dietary for Civilisation." Here the romantic strain is automatically relegated to the background, just as a Grenadier discards his scarlet and braid and puts on khaki before embarking for the fighting-line. It is an attack upon traditional stupidity, devoid of rhetoric and without trappings. Discussing state educational systems, he says: "Unfortunately, in spite of the vast sums spent on it and the respectable ability of those who spend it for us, we have not been able to get very glittering results. In most countries the product of all the schools has mainly been a socially unleavened mass of indifferent stenographers and clerks, and (of late years with the scientific programme) many millions of amateur automobile and radio repairers. Practically all our best men, from novelists to orangeade kings, practically all the men and women who are simply interesting and admirable, too obviously owe nothing at all to our schools and universities. Either they have resisted the system, or simply escaped it altogether." He goes on to say: "Most state educators are in the situation of gardeners who dig and manure heartily, without knowing if the crop is to be mushrooms or turnips."

Another and vitally important facet of William Bolitho's writing can be found in his article on "Van Gogh." Here he brings to his portrait not only a direct understanding of the painter's art, but a sublime comprehension of the processes of all true artists. I quote the last paragraph, which as an epitaph for a great man is significant: "But for this stupidity of the world Van Gogh was paid, as Blake was paid, by the inestimable advantage of being, until the day he died, artistically free. Art in a garret or a ditch can at any rate grow freely. No wish to please, no entan-

gling advice or encouragement, which has more often been destructive to original genius than mockery, ever came to corrupt his novelty or conventionally deform it. He was robbed of his reward, that is all: the least part of a career that is, after all, not entirely earthly."

There are, mercifully, no pseudo-mystical qualities in the writing of William Bolitho. His readers are never commanded to bounce off into the Unknown in search of nebulous half-truths. The world was enough for him, and he was content to live in it, love it, and laugh at it, very, very much for its good, but often rather too trenchantly for its comfort.

He died young enough to be called "brilliant," and not decrepit enough to be called "great," which is sad, because he would have enjoyed hugely that particular form of eminence, and I feel that he would have given his wreath of laurels a slightly rakish tilt, however old he was.

There is a word current in our language, a slang, rude little word, which covers comprehensively many major horrors. The word is "bunk." It typifies veneer, and smear, and false values, and although it is not particularly dangerous in its more obvious forms, it is perilously insidious in commercial writing. I mean commercial writing in the best sense, the Bolitho sense. The articles in this book are commercial in so far as they were written with the express purpose of making money. But nowhere in any one of them can there be discerned the most cursory acknowledgment to conventionalised sentiment, or the slightest compromise with truth. William Bolitho was incapable of seeing

Preface

*even the most hackneyed situation in terms of bunk,
and equally incapable of writing anything, for however large a sum, which did not flow directly and
clearly from the depth of his own perception. It is certainly comforting in an age when writing seems to be
degenerating rapidly into a social hobby, when no
shrill debutante can consider herself safely "out" until
she has published at least one novel, and when the con-
vulsive mental diarrhœa of Gertrude Stein can be
hailed as "progressive" and "important," to come
upon a writer devoid of modern clichés, affectations,
and sensationalism, and to realise that there is still a
standard of literature to which no short cuts are possible, but which must be, when attained, well worth all
the agony and bloody sweat which went to its achievement.*

*My mourning for William Bolitho as a friend is
nobody's affair but my own; but my mourning for him
as a very great mind indeed, should be shared, whether
they knew him or not, by all the young writers of this
generation. I say this in the full consciousness that to
some it may sound didactic and effusive, but be that
as it may, I want to put it on record as a completely
sincere and quite impersonal opinion.*

—NOEL COWARD

✦

Camera Obscura

✦

✦ 1 ✦

Sky Line

THE sight of the onrush of New York into view
out of the sea is not only superior to every
other spectacle in the world, but can never have had
a rival in the history of the world. My only hesitation
is about the nature of its precedence over London.
London, in the austere minute when your train from
Dover rises on a viaduct and overruns the immense
plain of smoke and slate roofs and asphalt alleys,
lifts the soul to a crisis that can never be duplicated.

Nor, I thought, equaled. But London is the marsh
of humanity. Its composite spectacle is essentially
undramatic, for it is full only of a despair at the
loneliness of man's fate, marooned on this raft of a
planet.

New York is a human mountain. While it is as
intolerant of optimism as the Himalayas, still it is
Height, not Depression. It has not less majesty of
magnitude and scale than the London mastodon. But
it has in addition the excitement of life. Which boils
up in that sky line. Architecture at last answers the
firmament back without being either futile or pathetic.

Its shape is like a Cathedral, as much as a man is

like a bird—that is, in no way except in geometrical accidents. The final nature of a spire is to leave off, however gracefully or gradually or reluctantly, in a final gesture of resignation. But these pinnacles piling up to the summit of Woolworth do not ever stop, even when they have reached a height that satisfies the eye without any aesthetic trickery. Their ascent is continued by light moving smoke, which joins the clouds on equal terms. So this beauty is crowned with its chimneys. The line of New York does not pray, or question. It states the case for life in an airy script of steam and anthracite smoke.

Do not, I pray, let your court-poet mess this discovery about with his allegory. As for the mass it (with the sea horizon) incloses, that is not a blank, a mere monotony that might have injured the elevation of the roofs. Inside and dynamically preceding, like the move of the acts of a drama, is a buttress work of planes, piled and slanted together for support, the set-backs of street blocks and skyscrapers. This mass, too, moves and lives, in huge shadows and lights.

It was a windy day when my ship came into Quarantine. Thick, shapeless clouds drove all the time across the sun. Every minute the façade of the city changed as its component planes caught a dazzling light, or were blackened out by a cloud. This city changed its expression, like a face. It smiled and frowned; it had all the emotions of life. Sheer perpendiculars, like wrinkles, appeared and disappeared. Steps and slopes were alternately chasms of darkness, or invincible dazzling buttresses.

Such is the gateway. I do not yet know whether it is like those Roman triumphal arches, practical jokes of a practical people, that lead nowhere. Or whether behind this sublime entrance lies the discernible beginnings of a new civilization, another and the greatest of humanity's sporadic excuses for existence.

✦ 2 ✦

Speakeasy

THE New York speakeasy is a stock drop scene like the masked fêtes of Venice and the coco palms of the South Seas. The best developed are in those shabby but unliterary houses wedged between millionaire skyscrapers that confuse all my ideas about land values. There is a stumbling, uncarpeted stairway with a stamped plaster ceiling painted to resemble bronze over it. At the summit is a wired door with a Judas-hole. If the eye that fills the hole is satisfied, this barricade opens on an unkempt, creaking lift.

Lawbreakers' charwomen are always feckless. This untidy, dusty lift enters the upper room without any more precaution. Here there are two opposite poles of noise, the orchestra of autographed guitars and, then at the further end, the bar. The tables are placed in a magnetic field around these two centres with a contracted dancing-room between.

11

No one dances—that is, with a partner. The man harassing the piano, of course, jazzes indefatigably on his seat and the singer has the conventional rhythmic fidget.

Behind the bar, over the heads of three or four layers of customers, are colored caricatures of the soft tissues of cabaret celebrities, faces of men, bodies of women. There is a photograph of a favorite actress in that most disadvantageous costume, a length of white chiffon, in which her body looks as unattractive as a blancmange trimmed with parsley.

These depicted people look sensible and straightforward, and a trifle hard, without any trace of the simpleton, without which art can hardly get on. Interspacing them are printed wisecracks all equally convertible into their contraries without losing sense.

There must have been speakeasies in old Jerusalem where they sold forbidden meats, ham and jugged hare. Here the favorite risk is gin and hard-boiled egg, or beer and bottled mayonnaise sandwiches. The gin produces a disagreeable uneasiness about the eyes. The beer has a curious, not unpleasant taste of pharmacy—between benzoin and senna.

The chief bar man and guardian is a mulatto with a cuneiform expression. Like most of his customers, it may mean that he puts too much will into his business, poor fellows who lose their tempers over a crossword puzzle.

Every one and myself have come here to be paid in amusement for the work of living, making money, growing old. It is hard enough—kings and poets with-

out number have testified since David—to wring out
of life our indispensable due of joy, even with the
grandest vintages, the most exquisite and romantic
women. Here, choked with the smell of toasted tobacco,
with nothing but this alcohol and these women, it is
unfair. The sexes confront each other across a wilderness of cigarette stumps in the ancient deadlock, the
men all looking for adventure, the women more practical. Both looks steadily express, without weakness
or irritation, the ungesticulant resentment of the
hopelessly welshed.

A little woman near the band begins to sing so impressively sharp that all heads turn to her. She has a
touch of the sheep in her profile, the inevitable mark
of the puritan wandered from the fold. What indomitable Don Juan could have the ruin of this born
school teacher on his soul? Now she has only the consciousness that she is damned to comfort her, and some
secret impregnable vanity about her singing, perhaps,
like most women who sing sharp.

She finished her song and left us with the unsavory
débris a sincere execution of a pre-war love ditty leaves
behind, like the kitchen sink after a dinner party,
lumps of eternity, tipsy cake, leaves of sodden gardens, the sediment of dreams. For God's sake!

I was quite sure this could not last. Just as half of
us had settled down to listen to further details of the
story the other half were trying to shout into us a song
began. It was not a new song. The man sang it in a
nasal whine, like a Moor relating the fall of Granada,
a manner much more exciting than any soprano, for

it addresses itself to the subconscious. So then we heard the only comfort there is in the world plentiful enough to go round—the pleasure of sincere art. It was late, but they served the wine of life at last, which sent audacious color into our cheeks.

✦ 3 ✦

Chicago

THE first view of a city, like the first meeting in a friendship, is probably the most important. But because both are too delicate to stand the wear of memory, like most of the other sources of our relationships, they are soon irrecoverably lost in mystery. If I do not quickly make a memorandum I shall hardly any more be able to see Chicago than my own features in a glass; that is, by reason, and not the eye.

But however I may inevitably deceive myself, I will have a prejudice about Chicago secretly at work under every intellectualization about it, because of the afternoon I first saw it. There was a grandiose fog over its suburbs. The approaching railway is very level, and the train is so steady that it makes only a whir.

All great industrial cities have surroundings stranger than anything in the moon. They ought to have connoisseurs, for every one is interestingly different. Going up to Chicago, even without the fog, and the immense smokebergs that drift like clouds

14

around mountain peaks, the monstrous metal vegetation of such regions, black and branched like trees carved out of anthracite, seemed higher and more bizarre there than I have seen before, even in Brooklyn. I have not the faintest idea what the purpose of any of these structures can be, being as ignorant of mechanical things as a Venetian of horseflesh. So none of their melodramatic effect is lost on me. But if mountain scenery produces poets, as they used to say, what incredible effect ought an upbringing in such regions bring about on the imagination?

But I can see, too, that under their satanic nobility, lit up by great glares, incensed by black and red smoke, set in sudden vistas of glorious street lamps stretching away interminably straight, their shapes are homely enough. If you can escape the hypnotism of their size, they are almost all domestic, even kitchenly; Titanic saucepans and colanders, and string bags on a stick, some of them; pepper castors; and oil funnels and strainers and ladles of all sorts. Possibly a mile high, as things appear to a cockroach in a pantry.

As the speed slacks, in the meditative and reverent way trains approach capital cities, it is easy to see the details. There is nothing very much more fascinating in the world than the back gardens and the lighted rooms of the houses on a great railway.

Great mansions, especially if they have no scandals, can be dull, with their dumb courts, anonymous trees that no one has ever climbed, and graveled paths that lead nowhere that matters. Slum tenements are better

15

to the imagination, but they are apt to be horribly confused, because of the instability of human life. But a working man's house, from its vulnerable back, as they always turn to the railway, with a shed, and a strip of weeds, clotheslines with washing, lights behind the blinds, a sagging fruit tree, very likely; this is a life, a story, a new Balzac, or d'Aurévilly. It may be an unwritten, lost piece by Shakespeare himself.

Now these Chicago back streets are the most fascinating in the world, and we went really very slowly. It is more a pity than ever that the benefactors who give us those thoroughly uneconomic albums of ornament and architecture are so routined. I would any day exchange my German folio of mediaeval guild halls, my colored plates of Syrian carpet motifs, as well as the whole of my stock of futurist projects, for an album of photographs of Chicago house design, from earliest times until the local builders became shy. These millions of façades will one day soon disappear. I have not to explain that there is no patronizing joke.

If these innumerable expressions of the past generation's ambitions, dreams, contentment and fancy are ever to be judged, it must be only under the mystical code of William Blake, or Henri Rousseau, the inspired exciseman. The man who would sneer at them, that is, would be stupid, as well as heartless. All styles, all manners of all styles are naïvely mixed in superb unself-consciousness—which anyhow is just the unique atmosphere in which all the arts can germinate.

Each man as he made his fortune, as he had made his life in this unparalleled time, made his home to fit his inner pattern. He fitted a Greek acanthus frieze on Gothic eaves, or built a Moscow onion turret on a farm basement, or mixed witty Versailles festoons with Swedish windows. There is nowhere a dull line, because each neighbor thought for himself; no monotony, because each front is inches out of alignment. Most of it is an eclectic borrowing, for there is nothing harder than to think out new architectural ornament. But most of it is modified by the poor memory of architect or owner.

There are untold miles of these houses, jovial usually, like the fantasies of fat and kindly men, genuinely queer often, and sincerely poetical sometimes. I do not suppose that any town in the whole world built since the middle ages, when the art of having different needs and boldly building to suit them was lost, is so romantically interesting as this ante-McKinley Chicago which flowered in the World's Fair.

They have kept stubbornly the prize piece of it all, that delightful Water Tower, in the midst of the skyscrapers, which, with its little brother opposite, is just a Nuremberg toy magnified a hundred thousand diameters: a wooden castle out of a box, with frowning turrets too small to hold a single man, battlements, escarpments, portcullises, donjons cut out of stone as if it were cardboard.

It stands among the soaring wonders of modern Chicago to this day, like Napoleon's pawky old mother in his glittering court. The lake line of Chicago is like a cotillion of Princes, dwarfing, but for this, its human makers. In front, along the lake, there is a vast jeweled carpet of flat fields, a whole milky way of moving lights. The sky signs are larger, or rarer and more deeply colored, than in its peer, New York. It is a unique majesty of Chicago that the smoke, in everlasting bursts from the trains, which continually pass in viaducts, under and over bridges, all along the front, as if the city were seamed with narrow gorges, blows and passes in front of these Titanic hieroglyphics of light, which burn and glitter behind them, half legible, at the wind's will, red and emerald.

✦ 4 ✦

Art the Great

THE Shires episode would certainly have been done into good, broad Greek if Herodotus had been around Chicago last week. It was just one of those anecdotes he loved, dense and curious, that subtend vast areas of information about the ways of kings and peoples.

This Arthur Shires is a baseballer and young. He has, for I have seen him, as you shall hear, that yellow crinkled hair that I know women love, without any possibility of explanation. This postulated, handsome boy, then, is full of animal spirits. The psychology of the Great Shires was the most debated subject in the sporting part of the city, so any deeper analysis

18

is arbitrary in the circumstances. In the course of the
spirits, during the last season, he disputed with and
then punched one of his managers, the no less irascible
Blackburne, a man getting into middle-age; and also
a reinforcement, with the two results: that he came
off himself scot-free, and got his name on the Chicago
front page.

Until this moment Arthur Shires in the great ball
world was entitled only to an "a" and not the coveted
"the." Sport is the shortest cut to fame, but this does
not mean at all that all ball players, or all big-time
ball players, are famous. Now, of course, to get in the
news because you have broken your manager's thumb
and severely hurt his rescuer, another ball player, is
not only an insecure fame, but a singularly neutral
one. For the day or two your exploit will last, it is delicately uncertain whether you are a brute to be elimi-
nated from the game for the sake of clean sport, or a
comical fellow, or—what Art Shires, with almost sublime instinct for publicity, made of it. The very start
was the first interview with the reporters. Asked as to
whether he had hit the White Sox's manager, he replied, "Ah, I wouldn't do such a thing." Asked, why
then the thumb and the black eye, he replied, "They
thought I was going to hit them. This made them both
so frightened and excited that they struck each other.
The friend was so bad that he bit Blackburne's
thumb." He added that every one on the team, and not
only every one on the team but every one in the league
was afraid of him.

This gave him in his second day's headline the title

of the Great Art Shires, and a further visit from interviewers. He now stated, "They call me the Great because I am so good a player. Mark you, this goes not only for baseball, but basketball and football. In fact, all games." He supposed he was the best man in the world at all these; as for music (he replied to one reporter), he had never tried at that yet.

At this point there appears Mr. Mullens. Mr. Mullens is a promoter, or rather, the promoter: one of those vast perambulating biographies the boxing world produces, with more anecdotes on him than a horse-chestnut has burrs in summer. Like most of the rest of his semi-hierophantic profession, he has made a living at it for generations, losing money all the way. He had almost agreed that boxing was dead in Chicago when this Great Art Shires business came along. Such a man understood the meaning of the situation at once. There is money in every emotion of the crowd; and here all of a sudden was hate itself arisen, a regular upas tree of hate, scorn, anger, best of all, exasperation, grown up over night. The whole hidden world of sport in Chicago wanted to see Shires killed. And Chicago, like an iceberg, is nine-tenths underneath.

So Mullens asked Shires what about it if he found a man who could exterminate him; and the Great Art, saying always the exactly right thing, stinging the mule all the way, agreed to meet, under rules, one Dan Daly, ball player in the provinces, reputed bully. Mullens on this whipped up a great crowd to see the fight. But it was easy, everything Shires said was so superbly right. I dare say that to a certain proportion of Chicago men during the week this was prepared nothing, literally nothing, their private and political and business affairs quite forgotten, was so cosmically important as for Shires to be thrashed into a jelly by Daly.

Daly, by the way, by this time had been adorned with the title, "mysterious." Mysterious Dan Daly. Mullens knew that a slight weakness in the perfection was that this Daly was not really famous, not quite famous enough.

Shires for these brief weeks was undoubtedly inspired. From an obscure scuffler, he had become as famous, I will not say as the President—as famous as Dempsey himself. A monstrous crowd came to see the fight. Shires stepped into the ring with "The Great Art Shires" lettered on his jersey. He won by a knockout in half a round.

And now Chicago boiled up. Why were there no sociologists on hand to study eagerly what was happening? This was war. The very fountains of corporate action were disclosed in eruption. You scientists might have learned as much from the next fight, which I saw, as geologists from a centennial outburst of Mount Vesuvius.

The second fight, the second convening of the mob to see the execution, exceeded in interest, learned sportsmen tell me, the Dempsey-Tunney on Soldiers' Field in emotional expenditure, in the grandiose spectacular, in, you have to call it, fun. This time Mullens produced to avenge the world a professional football player forty pounds heavier than Shires, a gladiator, a giant, a hero. Mullens could only pray that Shires would again win; he had positively Napoleonic plans for what was to follow.

Well, Shires was beaten, and the next day he was forgotten. I am not going to try to describe a fight for you, especially on Christmas day. My own sympathies leaped in a most confusing way. First settling on the good-humored looking giant, who received a terrible onslaught from the Great One in the first minute; then to Shires when he took those two tremendous smashes in the face from the fat man; from which his looks and his spirit probably will never recover. Then, equally, to both of them, like all amateurs, half dead through the last three rounds, so weak neither could lift a hand above his shoulder. The mob was the play. It was a death-trap of a place, no exits, every lobby jammed like a subway rush. Of course, every one was there, and there are some queer people in Chicago, in that hall made for five hundred and packed with five thousand.

But I remember forever that cry, that singular trilling cry, throbbing and whistling up like a billion startled sea gulls, that came when the boaster first fell on his knees. That, and in the middle of it, a white, ill face at arms' length from me in the storm, and his fist breaking the nose of another gang-man, when one single shot would have meant five hundred dead in the panic.

New York A. D. 3000

THIS season of the year, like a hill between past and future, almost forces us to look at the view. Even clods, and those so deep in daily business as to have the same mental behavior, are dragged back by memory now to make a sort of audit. We remember where we were at this time, what we thought, what we planned—the clearer, of course, as the distance is greater and the perspective enlarged. With melancholy that begins with a start, that 1908 jumps up at me in New York, 1929. Then I first had a hope of anything but a miserable and obscure life in front of me.

I was in a seaport which is almost the last on the south side of the world, vis-a-vis the cold mysteries of the Antarctic. But a hot city, at the height of the antipodean summer. There is a great settlement of Malays in that place, descendants of slaves, but now very prosperous and gay and picturesque. New Year is their great feast, as they are Shiah Moslems by religion. And at the stroke of midnight, which is what I remember, the guns of the forts give the signal. The whole population runs down the main artery of its quarter, women and men, with all their bands and in all their silks.

Well, that is a long time ago and a long way to have

come. But while this release of the memory, automatically associated with the day, makes New Year in its way as charged with emotion and as queer almost as Christmas itself, and both together a universal strategic stopping place for the soul, even Scrooge's, the time is also to feast the future. Speculations are in season, and to judge only from the immense prevalence of forecast literature ranging all the way from Haldane and Huxley and Wells to the pulp magazines this is one of the mental sports of the times. Is there any one who does not think sometimes, and now especially, what New York and life will look like in A. D. 3000?

All of them fascinate and dissatisfy me about equally. I have a special grudge, very likely, against the skittishness, the facetiousness, of a good many of the serious philosophers. Haldane's "Daedalus," still current, is a bad example of what I mean. I know of only one province where jocularity is so misplaced and deplorable as in high matters of science (the good old sun so many jolly old kilometres from the earth kind of thing), and that is in the even higher matters of art. But leaving that, as idiosyncrasy, the fatal manifestation of a thwarted sense of reverence, my chief objection is simple and logical. All the prophets work with the assumption that the future New York in seventy, a hundred, a thousand years hence will be, above all, new. I am much more certain that it will be, and visibly, very old. The further you look the older it will be.

There are two main factors in the misunderstanding. One is very innocent; it is the stress the unskilled imagination is biased to lay on the importance of means of transport. It is quite moderately certain that there will be, and soon, a large development of air traffic by various machines, quite possibly substitutive of those older ways we are more accustomed to; not only trains but automobiles. But the eye gets used to such things with facility. For a dreamer or a prophet to insist on the share this will have in the aspect of his future metropolis is as if some bumpkin out of the eighteenth century were to revive and then stare hardest and longest on the "L" railway we have, or as if the Kaffir Kinglets British Government officials of the Colonial Office were to take down the London subway to impress their visitors.

These things are curiosities, not wonders. Say that it is certain that flocks of flying machines will purr across Manhattan sky in 3000; it is even more certain that no one will look up at them or notice them; that many of them will be shabby, rusty, unsilvered, as dirty and used and banal as the subway itself. That, except for children and Kaffirs, will not be New York.

Moreover, you must realize that in every year the glorious young skyscrapers themselves are aging as hopelessly as the mortal children of men who made them. Of course a great number of them are going to stand. Some of them may be foredoomed to reach almost to the age of the Pyramids if they can survive the same vicissitudes of wars and natural convulsions. We see some of them come down each year and others taller replace them, and we think like some folk-tale nurse who should calculate that, as her baby in charge has gained each year so many pounds, therefore in a hundred years it will outweigh an elephant.

There are no such things in animate creation as straight lines of evolution. All our affairs and ways go undulating; rushes to city life do not, as Wells simply imagined, continuing straight on lead to the desertion of the country, but sooner or later, generally in a quite short period, to a reverse procession outward. Because there are twice as many cars as there were five years ago is by no means to say there will be four times in 1935, eight in 1940; but rather, according to all intuition of probability, none at all—one day.

And so you are now looking in the loud streets today at many structures which will last. Doubtless all their sisters are not yet born. Doubtless, too, the most magnificent will arise only in our old age.

I should like to look down Park Avenue in 2000 or 4000 A. D. some moonlight night. My eyes would have got used to the trivial traffic overhead, taking more trivial humans on their trivial affairs. It is strange that they will still be playing Shakespeare, reading him. But that great street by all urban and civic laws of growth—ecology is the lusty baby science that treats of such things—will one day be a slum. What if the inhabitants listen nightly to free music on the radio, or look at Presidents opening Congresses, or are fed by scientists with tabloid beef, or work at ten times as active machines? It will still be Beethoven, sometimes. The television frame will always be

26

cracked. The job will be rotten and the scientists' synthetic meals the same.

But the New Year night, out of one of the windows in the high fissured walls, looking out on the street which the rich lords and ladies of the past once trod in 1929, under the same moon, I am sure the same thoughts, after all, will come into the mind of some youth, listening and looking there, in old New York, as came to me in their time. The same old thoughts: unrequited love, perhaps; the strangeness of time and change; both the melancholy of there having to be a future and the cloud of recollection that the end of the year belongs to ghosts. We shall be the ghosts in 3000 A. D.; that will be the difference.

✦ 6 ✦

Subway Delights

THE mouth of the subway, entrance to the subterranean life of modern capital cities, varies according to geography. In Paris and Berlin it is decorated with iron lettering so ornamental that it is illegible. In London the endless tunnel ends in some mean-looking shop, without a window front. In New York the only sign at street level of the buried labyrinth is a frosted lamp, which might casually suggest a gas depot, or a hydrant head, or a traffic regulator which is none of the stranger's business. A mere wormcast on the sidewalk. Life likes to conceal its functional apparatus.

But these deceptive if not hypocritical mouse holes lead to the vitals of city life, through which the vast majority of lives are sucked and expelled daily. I have always found the caverns of nature disappointing. I cannot feel the slightest stir from the "fairy-like beauty" of stalactites, even in magnesium light; in everything but in size an ant nest is more interesting to the imagination. But man-made cellars fascinate me almost as much as roofs, and the best, gloomiest, weirdest cellars are to the great subway as a puddle to the Mississippi. The Catacombs of Rome and Paris are just theatrical in comparison.

One of the most exciting ideas of the young mind of H. G. Wells, before contact with dowdy people and banal ambitions had turned him into a shabby prophet of the commonplace, was that under pressure of a Martian invasion the survivors of humanity might take refuge in the inextricable windings of the subway cavern, where even superhuman beasts would not dare to pursue them. All down there is eerie and, in spite of all the glare and noise and crowds, very lonesome. The isolation from nature from which all city dwellers suffer more or less on the surface is absolute down there in the bowels of the earth. The dark places that a sudden spark from the rail lights up are worse than night, because they are eternally moonless and starless. Not a blade of the roughest grass can ever grow between those rails, even though no one has walked along them for a quarter of a century. No

spider will ever hang a web in the grimiest and most
forgotten corner. It is dead and empty as the realm
of pure brain.

But the air and the noise and the sights are unearthly only because nothing not the work of that
unearthly creature man enters in. The impure, tepid
atmosphere is full of man's smell—the unmistakable
musk of humanity that is as objective as the smell of
a stable, or a lion's cage, or a beehive.

The noises, too, are only unnatural and frightening
when our ears are out of the use of them, like those
the solar system must make in empty space as it
gyrates and rushes down the Milky Way; sickening
crashes, whirrings and spinnings, hootings that come
out of the dark; and when the opposite trains pass, a
scream that fills the passages like the passing of a
comet through the heart of a nebula.

At these depths, as spiritually profound as the floor
of the deep sea, human life glitters and flowers in its
infinitely attractive and unlikely way. The only spectacle of which the gods themselves never tire—the
coming and going of men and women, the tireless weaving of humor and tragedy, the good and the wicked,
the beautiful and the ugly, love and selfishness—is in
full show here, as it were in a prepared culture tube.
Sometimes, late at night, spaced out in dramatic
couples that whisper here and there on deserted quays;
at such a dead time that the noise of the lock of the
automatic machine some one pulls to get a tiny scented
envelope of gum makes complicated echoes. At rush
times, when the enervated, desperate crowds rush for

their seats down the stairs like waterfalls, and storm the home trains like shock troops in battle. When in middle afternoons you have room to sit, and space to meditate; and when jammed against a white enameled post, hurting and being hurt by the embedded elbow of your neighbor, whose face or anything but the back of whose hat you will never see again.

Even then, in such times of outrageous contact, when humanity is squeezed into a paste and loses even individuality of body for the length of the journey, it is possible, believe me, for those who live to enjoy life. The first effect of wealth is release from this daily process, and most of those who philosophize on the subway are released, so instead of the truth we hear nothing but their barren deductions and reason. The people of the private cars do not understand any longer the people of the subway; they misplace their sympathy and mistake their patronage. They pity the rush of the tired crowds—not understanding that (at any rate to the young) this is a violent, rollicking stimulus that works on the fag of the day as an unhygienic cocktail does more good than a plate of gruel. Some sorts of misery are better relieved by a night at a dance hall than by putting out the bedlight at 9 o'clock. Unless one is ill, the full spate of the subway is, after all, Life; the main current, the undiluted spectacle, any share in which is superior to all dullnesses, no matter how comfortable and rich; and surpassed only by the infinitely rare life of the spirit, which not one of those who waste their pity on "those poor devils" has very likely ever felt.

Comic Strip

Only the poet has any right to be sorry for the poor, if he has anything to spare when he has thought of the dull, commonplace rich. Life is a complete food; in the subway it is given away by the bucket. And when you, three-carred person—who are so tired of tea-time and your large but unqualitative friendships, your slow and tasteless rhythm of games—uncomprehendingly blaspheme life itself, try how it all tastes, new and real and vigorous, fresh in the vat of the subway, where the crowds re-enact twice daily, with the rhythm of blood circulation, the struggle for life.

How much more interesting newspapers are when they are read in jolts, gulped between stations, crumpled in the free hand. How much more there is to notice when there is nothing but a carriage jammed full of commuters and the advertisements above their heads. How much more savor there is in your girl's company when you come up and down from home in the rush hours.

❖ 7 ❖

Comic Strip

ALLOW a diffident foreigner to tell you that among the curious and characteristic native products of America, the trivialities such as compose the real originality and flavor of countries, the comic strip is one of the most to be appreciated. Nations are almost always slightly ashamed of their truly admirable idiosyncrasies; they all want to be distinguished only for massive virtues, which, even if they possess them in a remarkable degree, they only share with the mass of humanity.

A poor Fascist leader once pushed this vanity so far to me in Venice as to draw my attention impatiently from the architecture to the new docks, and commanded me to observe the young men busy there, in whom I could see only the shy bumptiousness, the scared vanity, the gang courage of ordinary young men anywhere—a depressing thing. "You ought to come to Italy only to admire our magnificent youth and modernity," he admonished. But I would not, nor would many others.

So without any critical insolence whatever, I confess the comic strip is a more interesting cultural institution than, say, the Mid-Western novel, or the mystical voyages of O'Neill *et al.* in search of God, or sophistication in all its branches.

Further, there is a kink in my outlook for which a terrible critic abashed me recently in a company by observing that "if Variety started counting points for what plays would be revived a hundred years hence you might come in the critics' competition." I had to admit even to myself that this Pharaonic norm, stultifier of all practical usefulness, does govern all my judgments. It is there too in this matter of the comic strip.

I have that fallacious feeling of absolute knowledge that a first edition of Theodore Dreiser will have only the value of its covers for a quaint period chocolate box in 2000 A. D., whereas the single copy known of three famous comic strips, say "Mutt and Jeff," "Andy Gump" and "Krazy Kat," complete from their beginnings, cut out and pasted in endless oilcloth-covered volumes by an invalid spinster of the epoch on an isolated farm, will have something like the value of the original manuscript, say, of the Book of the Dead.

First of all for its rarity. Ephemerality is one of the causes of rarity, speculative collectors should notice, not initial cost. The limited editions of to-day will never become rare, because no one will throw them away. But this certain rarity is nothing compared to the peculiar interest of the contents. Apart from the enduring work of authentic genius, nothing of the past interests us but its humanity, and the best quality of that is unconscious and unobserved. No one is interested in the cleverness, the posing, of bygone artists; the admiration dies with them. And so with their full-dress thought and doubts.

Like any undistinguished family, our great-grand-children will be interested not in our cabinet portraits but in the yellow snapshots. And where of all we talk and speak, the untouched detail of the things that amuse us, is the record except in these paper scrolls? As a mere matter of philosophic philology, in the countless balloons that float daily from the grotesque mouths of these marionettes (the Gothic carvings of our days) there is registered the most indisputably authentic anthology of our ways of speech, our very jokes. Here, in "Bringing Up Father," in fifty others which have run from time immemorial, is the exact detail, more accessible even than in the documentation of Leech, the family, social routine, of our lives—our amusements, our ceremonies, our attitude.

That is all right for the scholars. There is a more fantastic value which appeals to me still more. Of course I have no more pretentions to any kind of knowledge of this vast, oceanic distorting mirror than I have of the Talmud, nor than a strange termite of the street has in a white ant hill. These interminable stories are indeed like an immense system of burrowings in the world of fantasy and imagination made (in spite of the occasional celebrity of their authors) really by anonymity itself. In these illustrated palimpsests there are traced not only our jokes and our business but our dreams.

Take that dear cat Krazy. My imagination shivers at the learning and the research necessary, historical as well as psychoanalytical, before the reason for its special—Mexican, apparently—setting. But leaving that aside as vain as the search for the origins of Homer, or the connection between Max and Moritz and the Katzenjammer Twins, have you consciously noticed that it conforms to one of the highest ideals of creative art, known to all those who have not stuck in the mechanical theories of the classicists, like Ford Madox Ford, that here is the creation of a world habitable to the imagination because it is internally true to its own laws?

A heavy explanation for a thing all children, and every one who has ever had a dream in his sleep or read "Alice in Wonderland," knows *a priori.* Herriman has made a little world, queer, original, new, in which the imagination of millions has wandered and yet knows its way as easily as in Central Park—those flat-topped hills ; that jail, in its small, shuttered stillness, as uncannily recognizable as the "Inn of the Crocodile" by Gustave Doré itself ; all the desert roads and trees where Ignatz hides and discovers his bricks.

In this, the art of the comic strip at its best—there are naturally innumerable degrees of excellence and dullness in it—above its peculiar technique of drawing, as special and interesting at least as Egyptian hieroglyphics, is in the English inspiration. "Pickwick" started notoriously as a sort of celestial comic strip. "Doctor Syntax's Tours" and all the "Tom and Jerry" stuff of the twenties are much inferior to the Mad Count of Milt Gross.

But the point is that the highest genius of English story-telling, unlike the French, is rather to be sought in exactly the character that makes the best American comic strips fascinating, the creation of a world, true only to its own laws, where humanity may escape and disport itself, away from the other imposed reality.

And now I remember how often I have admired the narrative technique into which the best of them have grown out of the sheer pressure of daily inventions, the endless, beginningless novels or romances, unfatigued by any main plot. The dogmatics of the future, with that mythical and complete collection in their hands I have prophesied for them out of my own unfulfilled wishes, will have time as well as material to work out, I hope, the development of such a strong, folkish, primitively vigorous method of composing a story, alongside all the others of our day. I wish I had their luck.

✦ 8 ✦

The New Learning

THE curious incident of the "Einstein riot"— the press of 4,000 people to see a film on the Einstein theory at the American Museum, which led to some disorder, and the breaking of a showcase in the Amerindian section in the great hall—is worth a little more than the jocular comment it got from the leader writers. Even in itself the presence of so many people so ardently interested to see a purely scientific exposition of a theory notoriously abstruse and complicated is, at lowest, sympathetic. Things like this hardly happen anywhere else but in New York. You would not get a crowd like that in the South Kensington Museum for such a show. It is another of the fascinating little differences that make New York.

The comment as well as the episode has, however, a lot behind it. Alexander the Great bitterly reproached Aristotle, his tutor, "for publishing to outsiders the esoteric parts of philosophy." There is undeniably a snobbery, or more accurately an exclu-

36

sivity, or still more precisely a "snootiness," about philosophy which, as in the case cited, however, is felt rather by the mere alumnus than by the professor and scientist. It is one of those feelings which are complicated, which have never been reasoned about, and yet which every one perfectly well understands.

In analysis it is easy to see that this disparagement of the desire to know attaches to its mode only. No one, except a wild boar of the marshes, sneers at learning. But a great number of amiable people not only laugh at but are intensely irritated by any short cut. One more obscure manifestation of the Puritan instinct, which it is much easier to find in white races than any inordinate passion for pleasure. The Alpinist, and thousands who would never dream of crawling up crags themselves, too, feel that way about the crowd that take the funicular. It is wrong, a little bit funny and a little bit degrading, they feel, to want only the view, and not the climb.

Which climbless view is precisely what the 4,000 came to get. I myself am heartily with them. In fact, if I had seen the announcement, and if I did not suspect I had already seen the film in Paris six or seven years ago, I should have gone myself. The first task of the true sophisticate is to eradicate his sense of sin, not to repress it into twisted coils in the depths of his subconsciousness. I had a classical education, and while I confess I faintly despise people who have to read Virgil and Homer in translation—I also despise the feeling—I neither intend to abstain from my intellectual share of all that is being thought and done in other fields that interests me, nor, most decidedly, to take up an honest study of the elements of mathematics and the natural sciences. That is to say, I won't climb, but I will see the view. Or try to.

The dishonest rejoinder is that the real reason why going to Einstein films is deplorable is that no such film can give you any true idea of the theory, and that we will only go away either disappointed, or with a false impression, which will be extremely bad for our minds. But is not that the scientist's, the man's who made the film, and even our own, business?

The American public has always, that is to say for the virtual eternity of the last sixty years, been reproached as a whole for its exasperating desire to know, without learning, about things that are not its specialty. Of recent years this forbidden lust has, so far from dying out, shown formidable signs of great increase. The search for predigested knowledge, which wore out the tired smile of Europe, produces now the amazed stare. "Story of Philosophy" sells by hundreds of thousands, biographies clutter the bookseller's list, and are more successful than a love story in England, or a book of lay sermons in Germany, and not one of them pretends to be uncoördinated and unselective of facts.

Nothing seems too abstract or highly specialized for the Americans to want to have it explained. Millikan's researches go on the front page; the latest paleontographical pictures are in the Sunday rotogravures. With a barbaric innocence that has never even heard that there are subjects that a man must

never even think about, still less dare to confess his
ignorance by willingness to learn, the radio is jammed
with lectures on etiquette, so frank in their treatment
of the right behavior at a dinner party that it brought
a hot blush to my forehead this morning at 11 o'clock.
This people want to know—everything; and in the
only possible manner of such an enterprise, easily,
simply, preferably by pictures.

I hope they will never be snubbed or scared out of it.

For there was one other epoch of such a sacred,
hydroptic thirst for knowledge, the indulgence of intellectual curiosity, which is the only pleasure in life
that lasts and increases to the end, and that was the
Renaissance. If you tell me that the Renaissance dif-
fered and was more noble because it was primarily
eager for the grammar crumbs, and not the summary,
bread, I would answer: Sir, you have read Browning,
and yet you know nothing about the Renaissance.
One of the epicentres of that great convulsion was,
notably, the desire of men like Bacon to shear away
learning from the hands of a sect, to bring knowledge
into the open, out of the temples and speakeasies of
learning, where no one since the Greeks died could
penetrate without an initiate's ticket. This is the only
part of the democratic hypothesis I unreservedly admire or understand.

And this was not the end of the matter. It was this
appetite and its very partial satisfaction that was the
alternating dynamo of that glory, that civilization,
on whose mere savings we have been living until now.
I know that Shakespeare was never forgiven for not

having been to a university, that his encyclopaedism of erudition, gained no one knows how, is still felt vaguely illicit. He was in an age and a people—like ours—who rioted to hear about things they had no right to be concerned in.

✦ 9 ✦

Street Music

THE campaign against street noises is in many ways the best and justest of all reform movements. About all but one class of these abominable nuisances attacked, only a lunatic or a ruffian could disagree. All people, of course, have different tables of their aversion.

To me the execrated pneumatic drill is not the ugliest, by a long interval. Its crescendo roar is at any rate an honest machine sound. Since it is devoid of any emotion in itself it only fatigues my ears and does not arouse any destructive primary emotion in me. But the noise of automobiles, from the evil grinding of brakes, which is as it were the very voice of apelike stupidity itself, to the angry, insolent bark of the horns, the quintessence of all stupid and overbearing rage, the villainous impatience of brutish monsters, sends me into a reflex which is more wearing than mere aural fatigue. I am sure it encourages murder to hear one's self spoken to in that tone of voice: "Out! Out!"

40

they seem to say. I think it is even worse than the ferocious angry crying of babies, or even than the arrogance of a cur dog, two things nerves cannot endure.

But I am afraid that the first breakers of the peace to be exterminated will be just the street musicians. No one can be displeased with me because I must say something for them, for I am not so ignorant as not to know that, whether or no, they must go. This, therefore, is much more a premonitory lament for their inevitable fate than hopeful propaganda.

Yet to me (and to several of the most admirable people I have known) street music is one of the indispensable pleasures of a town. A town is no more fitted for habitation before it has been soaked in street music than a new house before a single fire has been kindled in it. Many must die in a town and many be born there before it is decently humanized—before its horizons lose their blankness, before it has an air of its own. In some way, street music coats its cold stones with a patina of the human and the supernatural, without a vestige of which life is unsalted, wherever it may be fixed.

De Quincey knew this about London, and all the terraces of his Oxford Street, where on moonlight nights he walked seeking his lost Anne, are full of gusts of barrel-organ music. London is to this day full of barrel organs; it is at least a component of its unique flavor. In Soho, the ward whose old name is itself a sigh, you hear them best, and in full autumn, breaking the meditative echo of the full roar of the town that surrounds these narrow streets by sudden bursts of strutting and strumming melody.

Even to-day London has as much other street orchestration as Paris, or Venice. I once heard an old woman at midnight playing the ancestor of all phonographs on the pavement outside Green Park there. And quite recently, sprung out of the huge mound of grief and misery of the ex-soldier, like a daisy in a cracked window-pot, there has arrived there a new piece of street music. I wish you could hear and see those strange English veterans, with their coats turned inside out—that too is a queer trick—who play their new spoon dance at Cockspur Street corner, under The World offices. They sing while they rattle their tin table spoons deftly and rapidly on their knees and elbows and up and down their legs, stooping and jerking themselves upright. It is a sort of island castanets, a shivering, natural cousin of the others, which carries across the whole road traffic.

In Paris, besides these organs, which they call with savor Barbary organs, they have many other street instruments. At the midday break the professional song-sellers come out, usually in trios of two hoarse baritones to one hoarse woman, and collect rings of midinettes around them to hear "realist" or amatory songs. The "Tiger of Belleville," or Maurice Chevalier's once latest, or Chanson Espagnole:

"Chantez ma mie, chantez toujours"——

Then they sell leaflets with words and music. It used to be for ten sous.

42

Street Music

And furthermore, the modulated cry of the rags and bottle men and the three-noted flute of the chair-menders that you hear from the bottom of the interior courts sometimes even now. It is as melancholy and fine in its way as the sound of the horn heard in the depths of the woods.

All of these sounds, these more or less professional sounds, tend to disappear, to be driven at any rate out from the busy centres of cities to their suburbs. There, in fact, it is best to hear some, not all, of them. For example, a German band, such as the one that stood at the foot of this skyscraper this morning and played "Heilige Nacht," very sweet and pathetic coming from such a depth, to me needs the ideal setting of an outlying park, somewhere on the fringe of the suburbs, unknown to any one but the few children and nurses that play there, as if they were lost; it needs those faint, effaced horizons, that air of exile far out.

But a great deal of it probably will never be cured, luckily, because it is not organized or paid for. Sometimes this is the best of all. The strange reassurance of hearing a piano played from behind a shut door, in a great labyrinth of corridors in a building where before there was nothing but the sound of your own footsteps. A girl practicing in the bow window of a suburban house, heard across its lawn on a tranquil morning. Many other sudden fragmentary harmonies that surprise you, aeolian arias, music like Ariel's in the air, and certainly very likely only tolerable because of its disjointedness and because it is quite disembodied.

There are now radio and loud-speakers. Again I have only a personal opinion; but to me this form of music is essentially and implicitly popular. It can be unbearable inside walls, or through them from a vulgar neighbor's flat. To me (and I speak of course only of the common apparatus, with a tongue of brass and a palate of tin) it should by no means be forbidden as street music, only localized to busy regions of the town, where the shops are gaudy and their fronts crowded, where women shop on Saturday nights in crowds. Then when it comes out at you there is a huge, indomitable life in it, very gallant, singing above the traffic like a giant, the resident genius of that place.

These things, and I again refer extremists to De Quincey and to Verlaine and to a host of others who cover me with their authority, are a great comfort to many who find life in great cities almost unendurably sterilized of beauty. Specially to poets, to those in love and to strangers, strangely enough.

✦ 10 ✦

Seeing Life

BROADWAY has a vast rich hinterland of interest, stretching west and east like an unexplored jungle. No one can boast he knows more than a few of the paths and clearings in this night country. The mere inexhaustibility of possibilities of spending an evening is one of the most powerful charms of such a city: Alice's underground world was itself not so rich in unlikely and unrepetitive surprises. It is true that the main part of the crowd seems to stay on the great high roads, Broadway itself, the jeweled theatres, the subterranean warren of speakeasies, the upstairs dance halls, the movie cathedrals and mosques. But if there could ever be a count one Saturday night —only the constables of Asmodeus, the devil who sees through walls, could make it—perhaps it is quite likely the population of pioneers and stragglers in the little places would be found equal to that which visibly chooses the dense main stem.

There are amusement places, and thousands of them, in New York which no one but a score of habitués have ever visited or heard of. There are others which have their faithful thousands, but never advertise, never have their names printed in the news, and which even the wisest pioneers could not place on a map. An evening out means to those a seat at a theatre you have never heard of, followed by a drink and a dance at the Blue Rooms, or Mick's, or Ruggiero's. Names as unfamiliar to you and as inevitable to them as those of their wives or boys. Well, this unending diversity of lives is one of the luxuries which only a mighty world-city can provide.

I went straying last night in some of these labyrinthine intricacies almost at hazard—that is, with a guide who claimed to have only a general idea of direction. I know that many rather smile at my explorations, because my fate and nature (which un-

fortunately have excluded me from participation, and
made me only a watcher) force me to get my pleasure
in a sideways operation, by deduction and not as a
natural share. So this evening I neither got drunk nor
excited, either in the English or French sense, on the
voyage.

First we went to the unknown music hall which is
situated, more strangely and romantically than a club
meeting in R. L. Stevenson's imagination, on the ninth
or tenth floor of a skyscraper. A grimy and incon-
spicuous entrance, an elevator door with the paint in
bad condition, sufficient to hoist you perhaps to some
feather broker in a small way, or the office of a hook-
and-eyes exporter, but so unlikely small that you are
sure you have come to the wrong building for a music
hall.

Nevertheless, at the top, at the end of a corridor
littered with crushed cigarette ends, is the desk, and
behind a great low hall. New York, now that I think
of it, is full of these unprepared surprises. Sometimes going into the deserted hall of a hotel, and
through quite desolate corridors, you come suddenly
upon a dining-room and hundreds of people at innumerable round tables.

Just as if you had pushed open a door on a roof
without knowing it, and there all around is a night of
stars, here was a full acre of audience, an army in
ambush. Nearly every one was a man—pale-faced
clerks, collared people, anyway.

Cheap shows all over the world have to dispense
with the kickshaws, and real vice is a refinement the

dollar places do without. Here they serve (with musical sauce, of course) just the plain nourishment of sex. The difference is, as I saw at once with the shock that a botanist has in finding a new orchid, that here in New York the fare was of an unheard-of simplicity. Even in a Chinese coolie's free and easy, the old dish has to be dressed up a little, and in Senegambia the innocent natives demand something more than sophisticated New York in this lost corner was supplying; glass bangles anyway, a real dance, something of art to help out the appetite. Now metaphorically, this was like a banquet for unspoilt Eskimos.

Consequently, all was of an unheard-of innocence, prearcadian, at any rate. A great, dark gypsy woman of middle age, with bright contemptuous black eyes, came out on to the runway over the orchestra, dressed in three triangles of spangles. Everything was reduced to that minimum beneath all the fears of morality which is not terrible, but almost irresistibly absurd. Even Havelock Ellis was a prude to this native ballet. The band played. She did nothing but jerk her hips in a highly perfunctory allusion, and then at intervals she would point to the covered parts of her brown, muscular, almost masculine-textured body.

It would be instructive for those who have confidence in the natural sensuality of men to watch this audience while she was doing her pantomime. I saw none whatever of the ludicrous and unpleasant reaction which Zola, for example, in such a scene would inevitably describe, or any of his innumerable, ungrateful imitators in "realist" literature to-day. In plain fact of observation, they were all, like I was, not in the least excited, but a trifle scared. Their smiles were half-way and sheepish, addressed not to the stage or the woman but to their next door neighbor alone. They were, in short, embarrassed, not fired; and strangest and most amusing of all, she herself knew this quite well, and eyed that herd of cowed men with the malicious mastery of a stout traveling salesman outstaring a girl who has to pass him alone down the long lobby of his hotel.

After this curious and entertaining spectacle, we went still deeper into the forest. I cannot forget that the exit was down a giant fire escape, and how its irons rattled under the hundreds of feet, and how the shadows were in the gaunt lights all the way down. Then we went to the just as singular, but of course subtler, enjoyment of a Second Avenue dance hall, where they served beer tasting like soap—perhaps the most depressing of bad tastes in the world—and where there was a most original bootlegger's wedding supper; just as full of incident and humor as the picnics in Mr. Polly. What a pity H. G. Wells, the best comic writer of the century, went to the dogs of social research. The father of the bride was there and made a speech. The best man made a long speech, and they all made speeches. The manager put a lime on them while they were talking; one of those lights which cast a stream of flickering stars. All through, one of the guests, a tenor, was trying to get silence so that he could sing Pagliacci's first song. And then we all danced, as Dr. Johnson's Panjandrum says, until the gunpowder ran out of the heels of their boots.

The Pony Ballet

THERE is always something worth seeing in the centre of a crowd if it has clustered for its own pleasure. Because, after all, men are worked upon by just as competent instincts as bees, and are fallible only in so far as they are intelligent. That is my pretext (I have no excuses) for always going to the biggest, most advertised music-hall show in every new place I find, whether I miss my obscure masterpiece of a play or not. The best crime, the best seller, the best music hall, these are the shortest cuts to the secret of civilizations which I recommend to diversion seekers on their travels anywhere.

The Ziegfeld show in particular is worth the same sort of attention great tribal festivals enforce everywhere, like the snake dance of the desert Indians, bath day on the Ganges, the Easter Pavanne in Seville or changing the guard at Buckingham Palace. Even on the steppes, at the back door of humanity, every savage knows that it is to human beauty what the Rue de la Paix is to other luxuries—the highest, most sincere thing in its own way. Any undistracted description of

49

its central nature must draw toward a comparison with some perfectly Eastern custom of Sultans and Khans —it is no use being bashful over the obvious fact that it is a market where we pay to see the best that a man who has the means and the taste for marrying for beauty alone may choose from. This is the outer hall of the (no doubt strictly monogamous) harems of the lords of our times, the millionaires, the sort of show a mere Turk would be bowstrung for peeping at.

These girls are a collection made by a connoisseur both by means of an active organized hunting through the whole of the United States and also through the opportunity which the fame of the business affords him of picking from those who have come to him here to present themselves.

The result is about six perfections, twenty or thirty very fine items, the rest still remarkable, but more or less flawed, who are set in the back row. That is to say, there are about the same number of perfect and nearly perfect beauties on the market in a year as there are emeralds, which, though it is incredibly more than the supply of authentic genius, is still something for the comfort of humanity.

Let us first dispose of any quibblings about Ziegfeld's taste, and this without any appeal to the general opinion of mankind, which is implicit in his box-office returns. The position is: about the half dozen there can be no dispute. I do not believe that an Eskimo would fail to ratify them; but that is a war that has been raging since Aristotle. Off this level I make exceptions. There is an auburn here, a snub nose there, with which I do not agree, but on giving his decisions the attention a learned connoisseur merits I began to see that most of the difficulties arise, probably, because when he had to choose among admittedly defective specimens, between a perfect body and an imperfect face, and the converse combination, he took the former. Fractionally, I suppose, the sounder.

Whatever the formula of this ecumenical beauty may be is only as profitable a study as squaring the circle. You have the whole range of poetry and proverbs on the subject, from the Song of Solomon to the erotic Spaniard's seven points, to choose from. The visible fact suffices; here is human beauty, underivatively admirable as a sunset, uncomplicated by costume, literature, with only its own prestige. I cannot imagine why its contemplation—and because of various mysterious reasons of photogenics only to be had directly, not from photographs, like the paintings of a master—is not as culturally esteemed as visiting the Metropolitan. In fact, the spectacle, outside the only ethnographically interesting songs and jokes of the book, is like that of rare porcelain. But superior to it as one of these ravishing bodies is superior in texture, color and life to any Ming.

Of course the sexual element in the pleasure of the sight of perfect beauty is very small, or, if you like, very much out of consciousness. These excellences are, as they have always been, for the class who have the task of power, whether grim barbarian conquerors, hereditary oligarchs or fat, cunning stock brokers. No poet has ever owned a peerless beauty any more than he has owned a Kohinoor.

I think as personalities they are unjustly misunderstood; Keats's Greek urn also was dumb. The curious, uniform, infinitely interesting expression of their faces as the close of each act sets them in apotheosis, which my companion piercingly observed "was just as if they were drugged," is not in the least stupidity, but a concentration, and only in that sense an absence of mind. You must remember that flawless beauty is a power, not less by a long way than any other sort of power, on equal terms with those to which commonplace doffs its derby without question—money, birth, office. But it is a potentiality, not an activity, and the natural expression of it is this semi-hieratical patience. They are thinking like the Dalai Lama is thinking on his throne, but certainly not our thoughts.

Imagine for yourself—no novelist nor psychologist has dared to risk the subject—the extraordinarily different life history, that dominant of personality, any one of these girls has had. From her childhood—wherever the mysterious whim of biology produced her, on a dreary farm, in a slum, in a garden suburb—her destiny, her treatment from her environment has been as different as any Queen's. A sort of awe has held off everything that brings merely human children to their senses. It has worked like one of those obscure protective devices with which the whole course of evolution is hedged about—how it would mess up ordinary social life if ever one of these happened to have a brain and a heart to match. We would have to put all the textbooks of politics in the attic.

So, reserved in an inward meditation on themselves as deep as a Buddha's with the same sometimes irritating patience, born to a destiny so different from the doubts and difficulties of the common lot that it is almost an alternative to humanity at all, they sit, or stand, or even consent to prance (for they are no more to be humiliated than peacocks and fawns) in a little trot, waiting blankly and unquestioningly to see what is going to happen next.

✦ 12 ✦

Willow Pattern

THE Bowery is nowadays in the dumps. There is no more badness or madness in its streets; everything is fallen into the dreary decay of an abandoned dancing hall, the litter after a low class banquet.

The Chinese Theatre is the middle of this detritus the coarse feeders on life in the nineties left, a huge unlighted structure with massive Ionic pillars ingrained with dirt, loathsome with some incurable disease that eats the stone away like mineral leprosy.

The never-swept steps end in barred and fettered glass doors like an enormous speakeasy. Behind them there is a light no stronger or clearer than the old gas jets, a foul anteroom and a surly doorkeeper.

Every one, except the children, in the Bowery is surly and hurt as if all the wives in the district had run away with young millionaires that morning. They are so out of courage that they do most things with their feet; kicking the doors shut, shuffling the garbage out of the shops. This doorkeeper opened the inner door in the same way, without an answer or another gesture.

Generations of dull travelers have spoiled with their descriptions and above all with their humor the naïve charm of the nonchalances of the Chinese stage. Funniness is the last horror of stupidity. Missionaries and tourists and illustrated articlers have so debased the sight of the long-haired stage manager who stands in full view all the time with his store of properties, tidying them and setting them ready for the next scene, his sudden darts with a footstool or a cushion to save the silk dress of a character when he sits down, that I am ashamed to mention them, even to notice them, almost.

Such was the custom in Shakespeare's Globe; such is not the custom evidently in the home towns white travelers in China come from, and hence the guffaws.

A Chinese play is as easy to follow as a captionless film, unless you are proud of slow-wittedness. Tonight it is an old heroic farce, a miracle play without the allegory. The evil Emperor, decorated with armor and weapons like an enameled crustacean, is on one of his campaigns, quarreling and ultimatuming, and then battling. The cymbals, which to our ears are the most characteristic and the only deplorable feature of the orchestra (like the asafoetida in Persian cooking), clanged continuously, like a battle royal in an ironmonger's store, for that is the way they underline emotion and excitement.

The actors in each episode enter by one silk curtain and exit by another. The first has a kingfisher embroidered on it, the other a peacock, just as in our nurseries a stork brings and an angel carries away. The actors have clear voices and a precise tradition of gestures, which they carry out, however, halfheartedly and in slipshod fashion for the most part.

There was one scene between a passenger and a ferryman which was exquisitely comic and so conducted that even the nuances of their conversation were comprehensible. I imagined even that I could recognize the rower using that mysterious Chinese word for "paddle," the most ancient word in the world, where the tongue itself mimics the splashing of the oars.

This boatman is afterward adopted into a grand family and made his audience—about as resilient as a plate of cold doughnuts—laugh to tears by that universal joy of humanity, a clown in high society. No one of these Chinese wants to talk. They simply want to be left alone. They are as scared of even the admiration of the white people.

How dreadful we Aryan whites must be to all the other peoples of the world; how infinitely more terrible and more real the white peril is than the yellow. Here they are huddled in daily peril in the very heart of the citadel of the unconquerably ferocious masters of the world, like mice in a tiger's cage. The man who is hawking Fook Yuen melon seeds and packets of spiced apricots tied up in a dried maize leaf that looks like dirt, why did he go through all that trouble and danger of entrance into the forbidden city to do that? Are there white men selling peanuts and hotdogs in Lhassa?

Here they all are together, barely half filling the littered auditorium, every face set in that peevish, worried look which we make mysterious, but which we would understand at once if we saw it on a bored, rather dull and scared child. They are the front rows of that endless army which could march eternally round the world without a break if the whole Chinese nation were mobilized and fed in numbers by its natural birthright.

The old mother race, we fierce, bright-eyed pirates and bandits, have treated her mercilessly enough. This old civilization has become all littered up, beyond the power of humanity to tidy up, like a palace or a library that has been used too much.

This play, these actors, are mere vestigial remnants, shards of rare pottery shining among a vast accumulation of garbage, disorder and decay. Still amusing those who are swamped with the utter meaninglessness of life, the innumerable crowd when they have grown so many that there is not even enough for them to eat. Art and love alone are imperishable and worth while.

Perhaps those two daubed characters on each side of the scene, in writing that looks like a map of an earthworm's burrow, mean that Old China, its rush and life, its palaces and gardens are fallen into ruins, but here still they are playing the old words, the old jokes, the old gestures to this dispirited bunch of peddlers and washermen in the New York Bowery.

One actress was beautiful and rare. Her name was Pat Lang So, and she wore glittering ornaments in her hair in the shape of things we, too, hold beautiful —flowers and stars. She played the wife of the slain Emperor in between the fooling, and sang his lament before an altar laid out with a tea set of silver. Her little, pure voice went on interminably in a tremolo while she dabbed her eyes with a green silk handkerchief.

I should like a little Chinese beauty to have mourned for me like that in a shrine on an inland mountain, surrounded by stunted pines and mountain grass that the wind bends at the waist. He yi yee, hi ye yee, with a flute to accompany her, her small, glossy eyes peeping out under her white silk veil like an insect's, just as strange and shining, unchanging and pretty.

✦ 13 ✦

Mei Lan-fang

MEI LAN-FANG is of the first rank. In that convenient if vulgar concept of sportsmen, he has a place in the world team of the greatest figures of the theatre.

Before the mind starts on that terribly tempting game of comparison, if it has to, you should be quite clear that convention and the program have not misled you as to the particular art in which, whatever it is, he is a master. I think myself it is merely confusing to call this "acting." I do not know the least word of Chinese, of course. But his articulation is so distinct that every syllable can be picked out. And there are very few of them. In two of his selections from his repertoire there are no words spoken at all. And so, purely for the sake of clear thinking, and not with the slightest intention of slurring the Chinese drama, I suggest that he (and his art) should be considered rather as ballet, even if it has to be a form of panto-mimic ballet which is quite distinct from any that we Westerners are accustomed to. To me Mei Lan-fang is above all a dancer; and as such I would not hesitate to put him in the very highest class.

To us who are used to the highly romantic ballet of the Russians, and the entirely romantic "chamber dancing" the Germans developed from the private prophecies of Isadora Duncan, through Wigman and so on, what he shows us is very strangely precise, measured, quietistic. An earlier age would not have felt this so much. For the most signal effects are simply those of all classicism, however curious the variation. Here is the masterful use of a body of rules, traditions and precedents, without the slightest appeal to novelty to help out; what for more than a century has been despised as "dancing in chains" and prohibited by

popular taste in most of the arts. You will first of all
with Mei Lan-fang be surprised at the effect of
strength and passion that there can be in the absolute
renunciation of originality. There is a power, an
ascetic power, behind these gestures which he does not
invent, but only execute; this single syllabled clarity of
expression of things done before which the wildest ex-
travagance or individual fancy cannot rival, even if it
is genius. Because it is a corporate total.

I think, perhaps, the tip of that charm is the utter
exclusion of the remotest possibility of a fake.

And now I must try to reassure you about one bad
impediment to a sane judgment and enjoyment of
this and all such exotic shows. The audience puts you
off. There is a certain type of admirer and enthusiast
who fatally attaches to anything that is out of the way
or new, whose unmeasured, or haughty, or, above all,
possessive praise arouses the most instinctive feeling
of opposition in decent people. You will find watching
Mei Lan-fang a great many of them, these "owners"
in the audience, and it will require the utmost self-
possession and objectivity to see for yourself, I warn
you, and not yield to the terrible temptation of saying
that anything such people admire must be nonsense.
The smarty, the arty, the gushing—they have all
adopted Mei Lan-fang; you have to be strong and
forget about them when you go.

He plays the women's roles. Apparently the Chinese
theatre has come to the quite defensible conclusion
that these should be the first in interest, as if "Hamlet"

should be "Ophelia" and "Othello" "The Tragedy of Desdemona." Some Chinese men, of course, have an almost unearthly beauty and distinction. There is another race of them in which every such claim is spoiled by thick, puffed eyelids. Mei Lan-fang is one of the latter. But you forget it as he dances. You forget also the harsh falsetto, if, indeed it worries you, who are accustomed to the subtle dissonances of modern music.

There are an almost infinite number of delightful things to see, and, as I said, the intelligence has a share besides the eye. It is not necessary to worry about the exact significance of each gesture of the pantomime, which some learned critics have made a great point of. These little symbols were no doubt introduced at first for technical reasons of stage management. But they have now become delightful in themselves, dance notes, no more obtrusive or prosaic than those of any European ballet. For example, the maids of honor in his "Vengeance on the Bandit General" walk around the scene to signify that it changes to another room. But this walk, above its little meaning, is a dance, a swaying, rhythmic measure, like a cathedral pavan, with the rocking, exquisite step, as if the actors were only attached to earth on a moving pivot, which is one of the chief verbs of this manner.

In this same scene you will see the extraordinary heights to which the Chinese have brought the art of make-up. The bandit, who rules Peking after the Ming dynasty, whom Mei Lan-fang rids the world of in the role of the Princess, is a symbolic representation in scarlet and lampblack of ferocity, cruelty, vitality, that leaves you gasping.

Perhaps of all that he does this Princess is the best —a study of beauty and art defending itself in desperation, as it must against the brute, like that most aristocratic and delicate of all fighters, the snake. Beauty has no natural arm against brute force but poison and ruse. But Mei Lan-fang is master of other roles and other arms. In his sword dance from the "Heroic Maid Cycle," I consider calmly, he has reached one of the supreme possibilities. You will see this, this translation of the play of lightning and the wind into terms of humanity. Also, and compare, the stylized sword fight with devils in the "Fox Princess" episode. By the time we European pirates arrived old China had evidently distilled war and fencing and battle into that receptacle which can contain all that is undeniably beautiful in it all, the dance. Our influence changed all that; and it is the fruit of our sins of taste and thought that there are to-day new bandit kings in Peking and, alas! no Princesses to stab them in their sleep in the holy name of true civilization.

There are uncanny voices in the air while Mei Lan-fang plays, scenery that glows and sparkles, costumes like poems about jewels. Yet there is no confusion about all this that is strange; it is the ghost of a great dying civilization that, like this great artist who brings us its memory, is, above all, clear and transparent and light.

✦ 14 ✦

Old Books for New

MR. LIPPINCOTT, Chairman of the Publishers' Society, warns the public that it is neglecting the old treasures of literature, and by implication or directly (I forget which) that it is too concerned with buying "the latest."

His statement is, of course, in itself almost a general truth; true, that is, anywhere and at any time. The public never buy enough old books. It is impossible that they ever should. And even its second half; the reproach about its taste for the new is not to be lightly denied, though I should prefer to put it in its only seemingly contradictory form—that they do not buy enough new books either.

Yet in America is a phenomenon which is not the least of this age and country, which few have grasped the immense significance of, that here for the first time in the world's history, since men began to read and write, there are over 200,000 people prepared to pay five dollars or more for a book they like. That "ceiling," as the French economists call it, borrowing the slang from aeronautics, will in all likelihood one day, sooner or later, be a million.

The real reason why Milton received only ten pounds sterling (was it?) for "Paradise Lost," and why even Balzac, in a time in which over the Channel Scott and Dickens and Byron were getting large sums, was paid only a pitiful thousand francs for "Les Chouans" (as I see in a note in the Figaro to-day), was mainly a function of the small size of the reading public of their day, and not principally the greed of their publishers.

But even their present number, and even the million surely to come, is not large enough in a nation of many millions of literates. So, academically, Mr. Lippincott's thesis is admitted.

I suspect, however, that there is still an interesting misconception hiding in his thought. Being a publisher, he has forgotten the vast and supremely important penumbra of the book world—the trade at second-hand. The amount of the sales of new reprints, Everyman, and so forth, is by no means to be taken as a total, but only, if even that, of a small indicative gauge.

Here I cannot resist grumbling at what seems to me a very niggardly fault of the publishers of these classical reprints, valuable and invaluable as they are. That is the small, miserly margins, which prevent these editions, even to the least bibliophile of readers, being anything more ever to them than a minimum of reading necessity. A library of these books is the breadline of literature.

Not only publishers, but authors themselves, are liable to forget that the greatest and most interesting of publics is that of the second-hand book shops. I will not say that until he has come to the dime book barrow an author cannot be sure that he is read. At any rate, the converse is true. Here is the public that does not skim; here is where, outside critics and fashion, poets are impeccably judged, and their good absorbed in the very marrow of minds. Indeed, what does it matter if such and such per cent. of your first buyers buy you only for display on their tables, or deny you a share of their time greater than just to flutter the leaves, which, if you are sincere, are written in the blood of your spirit? When you have been pushed off the boule table to the bookshelves, and gradually to the very top where the dust settles thickest, then is the time approaching when you can have audience with the attentive soul of a boy or girl. One rainy day you may talk your fill; that will be the day of the last judgment of rewards.

The greater public, therefore, is that of the second generation and the second-hand. The first sale is not so much more than the gate to this, to which the entrance fee, paradoxically, is half price. Perhaps it is seldom that a poet, for example, is ever learned by heart from a new copy. Yet that must be his greatest ambition and his greatest reward.

The first new book I ever bought was a Macmillan reprint of Omar. Since it is short, it had large margins. But by that time I already had fifty other books. I used to spend half what I got back out of my working pay each week on a tablet of milk chocolate, and half on a book. There used to be a junk market on the Parade Ground of the city where I worked on Saturdays, with heaps of coverless books on tarpaulins in the sun and wind, and sometimes it would take me the whole afternoon to select my nickel book. I think even in his Elysium Homer would be pleased to know he was read in an odd volume, foxed and scribbled on by the baby of the junk dealer, with covers missing.

This spiritual digestion, or adoption, is the real purpose of literature. I should hardly think it is sensible to suffer the pains of creation just for money or the mild pleasures of praise. But to have a chance to enter into the arcana of the thought of a growing and generous mind, to be grafted and adopted there, perhaps for the rest of a life, this must be the supreme delight. This is the deepest sense in which Keats has become "a portion of the loveliness which once he made more lovely" in the innermost memory of countless lovers' hearts.

I hardly believe that any one can really fall in love who does not know some poetry by heart. Without that, without the presence of these sublime catalysts, the emotion can hardly get beyond the stage of a tickling, an urgent greed, the sort of thing Dreiser describes so brilliantly. How can any one face dying without some of the prodigious lines of Shakespeare or Isaiah or the Psalms, whispering in his innermost ear in that noble, confidential tone? Or enjoy anything—sunrise, the sea, forests, moonlight—without tunes in his head to mould and capture the mere fog of unexpressed emotions? Music and poetry are necessary to human life: "A man can live three days without water, but not one without poetry," said the sometimes wise Oscar Wilde.

One of the most depressing prospects of a great deal that is being written at this time is that it is hard to see how it is to reach this echelon of readers. Pseudo-scientific, or "realist" dossiers on the life of spiritual paupers—this is admirable for shocking and impressing the present. Of course, too, there will always be a mass of vulgar and depressed people. But they seldom buy old books.

✦ 15 ✦

Fairy Tales

I felt a burning within me while I read the terrible heresies of Miss Mary Duggan of the Bureau of Educational Service at Teachers College, Columbia University. You remember that Miss Duggan condemned the traditional nursery rhymes, and, by implication, the whole realm of faery, in the life of children. I know how squeamish every one is to-day about the word, so I hurry to say that my authority for its use is that ever up-to-date, unwhimsical author Walter Savage Landor, and I can prove it.

Miss Duggan then, after making the strange statement that children so brought up would end by becoming readers of G. A. Henty and Zona Gale, ends with a perfect epitome she has invented of all the nonsense—dangerous, too—concocted by her school of fancy and imagination, in an abominable story of "A child named Peter, who ate'n ate'n ate spinach,

66

until he was strong enough to lift his little horse Trott Trott high over'n his head."

I will save my indignation at this to criticize the choice of authors in her warning. Why Henty and Gale? The first I cannot believe she has read. I thought this perfectly unimaginative, well meaning, moral, matter of fact Dugganist, in any case, had long been forgotten; his indigestible masses of suety history, dowdy description and moral adventure long subsided into the primeval pulp to which all dead books return. If she had said that children reared on the ancestral sap of Mother Goose and Grimm might later on take to Sax Rohmer and detective stories, it would be more likely. For such are certainly fairy tales for adults, complete with crooks for dragons, and falsely accused witnesses for forlorn Princesses. That is their charm, and that is their defense. It is pretty certain that the man who cannot read them, at any rate to the inability of disgust, and who, the same person, delights, let us say, in Wells on marriage, or Galsworthy on love, is without knowing it utterly unliterary. The root of the matter is not in him.

Now, as for that story of spinach, it seems to me masterly in the way in which it combines every obnoxious idea and error in the education of a child; the nauseating "boy-talk" in which it is cast, likely to rot, permanently, a sense of good or even clean style; its inherently vulgar ideal. I do not know what a child reared on such stuff will read when it grows up, but I suspect it might well sink so low as to enjoy the spectacle of Greco-Roman wrestling. And, of course, thus early it would have implanted in it a fear of the most dangerous bugbear of modern life beside which all witch's and night fears, even the most demoniac, are sprightly—the spirit-destroying obsession of the fear of constipation with which the modern world is hag-ridden. Why else spinach? Why else should a child by a cold and unfanciful life, unredeemed by any poetical motive, be led into thwarting its most sacred innate abhorrences and take to the food of the ox?

The deep, irreconcilable opposition I feel to the precepts of Miss Duggan's school, however, is far beyond any compromise on the terms of such a fable, in whose criticism, of course, I have been very unfair. I am a die-hard partisan of tales of wonder and imagination for children, even to the full distance, even, that is, and I almost said above all, of Grimm and Musaeus. In the first place, I must hurry to say, I do not propose this regime for all children. One of the most vitiating errors of all talk on education is just that every opinion held is supposed to be a general one, for all children, for all schools.

I do not believe that there is a finger count of general axioms in education. I do not even pretend in the least that this or any other suggestion I make is good for the majority. I have nothing to do with the majority, who synonymously are destined to be mediocre men and women. But for those who have the courage to hope that their children may become members of an elite, economically and politically perhaps, spirit-

ually certainly, I urge that the education of the won-
der-tale is of the greatest importance. Perhaps it is
even of greater importance than in the days past of the
Goodchild family, the days of the "Fairyland of
Science," of Arabella Buckley and the soul-destroying
allegories of giant Laziness, the elf Neatness, the
dragon Bad Temper, to which stuff nearly all the
stupidity of the Victorian age can plausibly be attributed.

For then, at its lowest, the child had the conceptions
of religion to keep its soul alive under the detriment
of these horrors. Nowadays when so many children of
intelligent families have not even this corrective, it is
necessary to remember that virtue is a concept that
cannot be based on utilitarianism or reason alone. I
do not personally regret that the idea of heavenly rewards and punishments may be fading. But it must
be compensated for by an adequate assistance of that
other, older, concept of fairyland, whose basis, in all
nurseries from Papua to New York, is that virtue has
a princely beauty, and that beauty itself is a virtue.
And above this foundation of natural granite is the
roomy fabric of the world of wonder and surprise.

The imagination, I dare say, is the minimum
faculty of humanity, socially, personally, cosmologi-
cally, and those who debar their children from their
birthright of entry into its regions, even to its wildest
and remotest corners, are condemning them to something less than full human destiny, fitting them, by the
too early corruption of the commonplace and the
matter of fact, not to become robots, but the valets of

robots, the stable boys of airplanes, the hostlers of engines.

In such a subject there is a side road to be explored and explained at every paragraph, not one of which we can here explore. One, however, however hurriedly, must have a word. Do not think, please, that I want to increase the sales of any Peter Rabbits, or Tommy Mice, or any such part I can see of the vast quantities of bunk literature, adorned with insincere art school illustrations, with which the shops now are stuffed. Grimm, with his witches to teach the child the great truth that the world is a wonderful but not a cozy place; Andersen, some of the Lang books, above all, perhaps, the Arabian Nights—such are the safe diet for those who have not time or inspiration to taste for themselves. I almost forgot Uncle Remus and Mrs. Nesbit, Clemens Brentano and Wilhelm Hauff. Let them know these by heart.

✦ 16 ✦

Believe It

HERE is a book, like a boy born with a caul, doomed to have strange adventures. Long after it is sold new and net—which is, authors forget, the least important part of a book's life—it will drift about the world second-hand, wherever curiosity and English occur together, turning up in the forecastles of ships, in dentists' waiting rooms, in small town auctions of small home effects, in barracks and camps, and in temperance hotels, where traveling salesmen are given special rates.

Wherever it is until the paper crumbles and the strings wear out, it will automatically make the eye stop and the hand reach out, and it will never stay in the 10-cent box outside the used bookstore more than a day. Such books are rare. They are a sort of currency of reading. A list of them would be amusing to compile and meditate upon; I should like to make one myself one day.

The real comparison of Ripley is not at all with Marco Polo, nor with Sir John Mandeville, which several of his friends have tried to impose on me. Traveling to him is an accident, as it was to Herodotus, a mere supplement for a lack of material, and his real predecessors are the great bookworms who tunneled the dust of libraries for their prey. The analogy is the "Anatomy of Melancholy," Pliny's "Letters," Hone's "Books of Days," Montaigne, the celebrated Brewer of the "Dictionary of Phrase and Fable," the country almanacs of Europe, and many others I could remember if I had the time, whom, by the way, I recommend to Ripley as mines I suspect he has not yet thoroughly explored.

All these, no doubt, represent the learning of curiosity, and Ripley is not learned. It would be better if he were, as it would often enable him to see the full meaning of a story he has found, or round it out in its full beauty. But I would only wish it, if I were certain

71

it would not blunt the razor edge of his curiosity. That is the main thing and in this, the most important, he is the equal of them all.

He is rightly excited to discover that "manna" is found in the branches of the tamarisk and sold in the Holy Land, where he tasted it. But he is not aware, and it is a pity, that the substance is sold in great quantities in France, where it is—and this is a sufficient reason why his surmise that one day it will be sold in American candy stores is unlikely—the normal, safe aperient for infants and old people.

The book the fantastic Gustave Leblair read daily at the Bibliothèque National in Paris all his lifetime could scarcely have been the life of Saint Apollonius of Tyana, but all the same that is a fascinating book and wonderful, which would delight Ripley's own heart. Also, believe it or not, Gambetta, the great tribune, was even more renowned for his optimistic and enthusiastic stories about himself than for his "ability to repeat all the works of Victor Hugo, word for word," let alone backward.

But I am not making a dash for the honor of the only man successfully to confute one of Ripley's items, but only unconsciously exemplifying the reaction which is one of the most delectable charms of his work on its readers. Which its very title shows that he counts on. He is not merely retailing empty wonders to make yokels gape. His research is for the very highest type of curiosity, the unbelievably true, and when he has found it (as in that sublime "Lindbergh is the 67th") he knows it by the tribute of protests. Be

72

sure he is always waiting with his authority in his hand, like a club, at the top of the stairs.

In this way "Believe It or Not" has a role which far exceeds and counteracts that of many a hundred literary upliftings and smartnesses, which I am rebuked for not troubling about. Why should I give a whole column to such a trifle, when I never even acknowledge receipt of Humbug and Hokum's account of how they think the world ought to be united for dullness? Because this one pricks the sluggish mind and coaxes the doubtful one to a true realization that the world and life are miraculous and interesting.

There never was a time when the illusion of banality was stronger. Literature and religion and even science seem to be united to promote the great illusion of ordinariness and dullness, to put us and keep us in that stupor into which our constitution makes us so liable to fall, in which nothing but the everyday is visible, nothing but the commonplace real. At any rate in the middle ages heaven and hell were near, and that is infinitely more true than that they do not exist. Beginning in a marvel, ending in a marvel, living out a story full of the most outrageous surprises, hazards, shot through and through with the supernatural and the extraordinary, creatures of fire and blood and air every one, we are hypnotized to forget even that we live on a wandering planet whirling through immensity. The very quantity and magic of the instruments which the brains of a small group are shoving into our hands bemuses us, rather than elates us. All, except those who escape by being too low or too high for the gas, are stupefied into boredom. The most malignant heresy, the most idiotic falsehood, that a brick is more existent than an emotional state, than the least overtone of a poem by Shelley, is taught as *a priori*.

Ripley's little book will save you an hour or two at any rate from this life-destroying fiction. The world is ruled by law, certainly; read him and see with what wild eccentricity, what infinite good spirits, what fantastic jokes, it is administered. Read of fate's jokes in Ripley; they will cure you of ever disbelieving in her again; read of her coincidences and then laugh for the rest of your life at the naturalist school of fiction which has excluded them from the picture and still claims to be realistic. This is a pamphlet for truth, for the incontrovertible truth that life is miraculous, breathless, and good to live; that anything but the dull expected is possible, and only the marvelous, predictable and sure, and inexhaustibly enough to go round.

✦ 17 ✦

Rekilling No Murder

TO write the biography of a great artist is an ungentlemanly job. Unless it is not a mere praise book, it will have to contain as many scandalous secrets as possible. On this "human interest stuff"—a phrase

74

which is a confession and a misanthropic commentary
—the fate of and the reason for the book will depend.
At the end, of course, there will be a chapter "summing
up the message," with several paragraphs explaining
that one must never forget, &c., that in spite of everything. . . . For, unlike all other biographies, this
species has to pretend to defend—the only excuse for
so betraying an artist is that he was a great one.

I do not myself think this excuse is valid. Kings,
conquerors and criminals are public servants and after
their death their lives fall into the public domain. But
there is rarely anything interesting in the life of a poet
that he does not want to conceal.

Thus, how far does it clarify or embellish the
"Fleurs du Mal" to hear Baudelaire was impotent?
What right have you to read, or any one to write, that
Dickens had rows with his wife; that Carlyle, Ruskin
and Shakespeare were this and that with their wives?
How wise, or lucky, or both, Shakespeare was, anyway,
to have lived without leaving more than a birth certificate and two or three bad signatures as the sole material for the diggers to disentomb!

This life of George Meredith by Robert Esmonde
Sencourt, is a sort of test case. It is done by a scholarly
man, a writer who neither annoys nor unduly stimu-
lates you by his style. It may quite possibly be true
that he consciously thought he was doing Meredith a
service and duty to the world by publishing it. Certainly it is interesting—and the most interesting part
is the complete satisfaction of our lewd curiosity about
this aristocratic, secretive man. Meredith, then, as all

the old literary gossips used to mutter to you, was the son of a tailor in Portsmouth—a very superior tailor, a dining-out tailor, a tailor that called his customers sometimes by their Christian name, Mr. Sencourt volubly assures us.

That was Meredith's secret, and its divulgation has two effects on me. First, that he was right in hiding it. It would never have done for little Oscar Wilde to have known this about the creator of the highest bred heroes and heroines in the whole of literature since Homer. It is no use your invoking the sacred democratic norm. If his father had been a farmer, or a traveling showman, or a juggler's laborer, that might have passed. But not a tailor—not for Meredith. And so, in the second place, you ought to feel a horrible embarrassment that this private matter was not respected and a humiliation at having listened to Mr. Sencourt's blabbing.

For, as with the most extraordinary incomprehension the author recalls in his preface, George Meredith "was violently opposed to the idea of any one writing his life." Sir James Barrie, his executor, has always because of this refused to allow the documents in his charge to be used for the purpose. I think I remember Mrs. Meynell once told me Meredith destroyed as much as he could all traces of his past to make the enterprise impossible. Mr. Sencourt goes on to say it was therefore "Meredith's own fault" that no biography has until now appeared.

But the great, savory item, the great secret that has been taken from the hand of the poor corpse, the

ultimate product of the coffin-plundering, is the story
of Meredith's first marriage. She was the daughter of
Thomas Love Peacock, the illustrious author of
"Nightmare Abbey" and "Headlong Hall," the intimate friend of Shelley and Byron—a man whom, by
the way, Mr. Sencourt most exasperatingly under-
estimates and patronizes. Now, this Mary Peacock,
after giving George Meredith a son, ran away from
him. A most unhappy, unlucky woman, pre-Victorian,
obviously Godwinian—Shelleyan probably. Worst of
all when she came back, cast off, and asked to see her
baby, Meredith refused, even for an hour, even for a
minute, even from across the garden fence. And she
went mad and died in an asylum.

How any person with sane human feelings can imagine that the abominable uncovering of this dire business can "help to appreciate the full beauty" of
"Modern Love," the poem cycle dedicated to her in the
first married days, escapes me completely. By reaction
at the monstrous indiscretion of which in his grave
he has been victim (with the complicity apparently of
the son by his second wife) the revelation cures the
wound to our sympathy toward him that is caused.

Poor Meredith—worse treated, in spite of all the
precautions his shame took not to be uncovered, than
Shelley himself by the difference of talent between Sencourt and the arch André Maurois, whom Sencourt
claims as master. Poor poets all of them, dug up by
industrious, clever, obtuse men; their poor and bloody
secrets tracked down in registry offices, through lawyers' archives; their love letters thumbed through,

printed and commented with delicate humor; their pretensions misunderstood or divulged; their linen baskets and washing lists gone over—their very bodies in their defects exposed to the public on the stage of a dedicated, full-length, dust-jacketed book, complete with hors texte portraits.

So we now know, for no one can any more keep his eyes away from such books than abstain from glancing at the spectacle of a horse which has broken its legs in a street acident, that George Meredith had a rather unattractive family; that he once wrote of his first son, Arthur, Mary Peacock's son, that he had grown up to be "a short man, slightly mustached, having a touch of whisker, no intellectual athlete"; that he had a collection of friends who sound awful; that he drank a great deal and loved the company of his servants; that he was notoriously enthusiastic about beautiful women on first meeting, but that we are guaranteed by Mr. Sencourt that there was nothing more than platonic in these matters; that, as any of his servants could have told you, he used to rag his children unmercifully. . . . For the rest, and the things that Mr. Sencourt could not find out—a man who destroys all his papers must get a good start, even if his own children join in the hunt—and the illumination they would throw on his works, we will very likely have to wait for the great exposure on the Day of Judgment, if, indeed, for Meredith and all such mistreated poets there is one.

> ". . . For they are but men
> And rest eternal sorely need."

18

The Medium

THE medium occupied a high-backed, tapestried chair. On his right side was the hostess, who had arranged a little table so that she could wind up the gramophone and change the records without getting up. On the left of the medium sat the first business man, who looked more like the Colonel of an English yeomanry regiment, handsome, tailored, repressed, in a comfortable chair. On my left was the Irish traveler, whom a lifetime of adventure had confirmed in the habit of romance. Then, next to the fire, opposite the gramophone, the other business man, warming his hands mechanically.

The medium took a long sip of either gin or lemonade out of his Venetian glass tumbler, set it down and asked that every one should put both feet on the ground for a while, owing to the currents. He said in a matter of fact way that he was a deep trance subject. Some mediums were light trance subjects, he was not. First of all, Frank would whistle. And then probably White Cloud, who was an Indian chief before he passed over, would take control.

This medium was really a very ugly man. His lips were extraordinarily thick and pursed, with a thin, reddish mustache laid on top. He wore a ruby ring, which is a jewel ginger-colored people should beware of. Tiny blue eyes, set and sore.

The first music was not what he wanted. So the hostess changed the record with her long, white hand. Then the medium gripped the ornamented arms of the chair; his fingers were short and thick and he had hardly any nails. He put his head back and his tongue pushed out as if he were half throttled. Frank began to whistle—quite good whistling—along with the gramophone, the hostess looked over to him quite friendly and at ease, and asked him if it was all right now.

This whistling was a strange, questionable thing in that sleek, warm room. The mind refused to decide its nature or its origin, and refuged itself in imitating the strictly banal attitude of the adepts. We listened politely and a little impatiently to this sound coming across the division between the living and the dead— which might equally express either a belief already worn into a commonplace or a conviction that took trickery for granted.

The spirits were disappointing. White Cloud was perfunctory in his introductions, and even in his stage-Indian accent. I had the impression which all the records and evidence always give me that the unseen world "hedges." That by a combination of the inexplicable and the inadequate in all its manifestations, the conclusion never moves one way or the other from doubt. If a name is called which could not possibly be known, the message is always so empty, so unspecific, so superfluous and uninspired, that the soul that has jumped forward eagerly to believe is left suspended all the same.

The Medium

One by one, strictly in turn, the voice went around to each in the half circle, like a priest administering the communion. The sight he announced and interpreted was detailless and poor; a tired and dispirited Red Indian pointing his finger to a little glum group of ghosts: a plump, blue-eyed woman, uncertain of her name; an old Jewish grandmother, still thinking of Purim cakes, her husband with a black caftan; a little girl, a tall man named William who insisted in vain on being recognized by me, an unidentified young man with a sore leg, all standing somewhere in a perfectly featureless landscape, waiting for a chance to say to us something with no more individuality or warmth of emotion than the greeting on a Christmas card. Dull, dutiful visitors, like a flower mission after a tiring round of the hospitals.

The fault was not in us, I swear. It was the dead who were cold. Each of our business men trembled with eagerness when the slightest clue of a name gave him a desperate chance to believe that some one out of the past was calling. The baldest of good wishes, recollections so insignificant that they could only be recognized by a long searching of the memory—this is all that we received. I am watching over you. Do you remember Elizabeth? She's here too. You just remember her; she was not exactly a member of the family, but very near at one time.

Not a kiss, not a sob, hardly a limp handshake; and not the faintest trace of realization of the horror, mystery and anguish of such a meeting, across a barrier which has held up a million years of human despair and sorrow.

In the middle, somewhere outside, a brass band began to practice carols, which of all hymns have the heaviest load of memories. A great many people can remember every single Christmas they have spent, right back to the limits of consciousness and childhood, and carols bring it all up.

The medium stirred and muttered at this. Remember that there was not the faintest air of fraud or incredulity in the thing. The face and the moving lips were those of a sick man, a suffering man; there was a sort of birth going on, not a pose.

The Indian was as real as a club bore; his invisible companions small-town tourists in space. Unimpressed, unfeeling, profoundly unattractive. I could imagine them hanging about, feeling vaguely hungry and wondering what time it was.

At last, after we had regretfully and kindly refused to recognize a series of spirits who tried to pump us about their identity, the seance ended. The medium came out of the trance through the same unpleasant symptoms as he went in. The beautiful face of the hostess lost its expression of mysterious patience. No one had tried to come through to her; but I could see she had some reason not to be in a hurry. The lights banished the cheerful flicker of the fire, and coffee was served.

I was inclined to believe that we had spoken to spirits; disappointed in them. And sorry for us all, whether the soul is immortal or not.

19

Jung in Shipwreck

HARDLY any one still wastes time looking for the philosopher's stone or the elixir of life. But the old game of scientific mind-reading still goes on; in short, it is more ardent than ever, since Freud, Jung and Kalges revived the subject. Hence the sale of all these books about What Is Behind Your Front? which promise, just as Lavater did with his Types of Faces, and the Phrenologists, to let out a methodical way of getting at other people's ultimate secrets of character, and even our own.

I have just been through the latest of these and am in the position of being convinced, without believing it, that I am an extremely introverted intuitive who has taught himself a minimum of extroversion. As I also look like Nietzsche (without his mustache, if that is a possible thought), I am in the corner of the chart of types with Edgar Allan Poe, Beethoven and Immanuel Kant, and therefore should do well as a laboratory assistant, great artist, or motor salesman in a cultured and aesthetic milieu such as Palm Beach.

But I would not risk either love or money on it. It is not only because Professor Jung, the ultimate source of most of these discoveries, already has fallen into an amused discredit in his own German academic circles, where they ought to know. Nor because the lists of questions by which the modern mind-readers arrive at their conclusions are not acute and even super-detective. They are, and when their results are combined by an ingenious system of point counting they certainly reveal something that is interesting and likely to be true. These psychoanalytical people are competent rat-catchers of consciences. But when they have secured their result they are quite mistaken about its nature, and dangerously overestimate it. This is not the Self that runs into their cage in the end, but only the prevalent mood of the self. That is not such valuable information; in fact it is just an amusing restatement of whatever who had bought some experience knew already.

This Extroversion and Introversion, in fact, is not a classification of Selfs, as is advertised, but merely of methods men have of getting their living and their life. Tactics, good, bad and unsuitable, for dealing with likes and dislikes, which latter are the result of a complex of health, age, education, reading, experience.

The "extrovert" has discovered that he can get what he wants by joining, belonging, expressing. The "introvert" has not found out the trick, or he does not want to, because the method does not give him what he wants. It does not even require a crack on the head for one to shift his category: a good sound snub, a scandal or simple boredom will make one out of the other almost instantly.

Introverted, Mr. Dreiser became as noticeably extroverted as soon as "An American Tragedy" went into its tenth edition. The first wrinkles, the coming of a second chin, change inveterate gold-diggers often into romantic idealists; many shows now running on Broadway I guarantee to change the purest sensationalist into a sensitive dreamer shrinking from the pleasures of this world. Such changes are the staple of the novelist. They dispose of the practical claims of the system, which merely teaches you how you affront life, not what sort of woman or man you are.

For this we have to stay in the old knowledge, the nearly instinctive manipulation of "mean" and "swell." In the crucial moments of life, falling in love, hiring an employee or taking a job, in battle or fire or shipwreck, that is the only thing you have to know or want to. The ship heels over, there is green water in your cabin. The time has come to find out the ultimate things: which is the front and behind of the life jackets? what you are? what the others are? And the answer will cut right across all the psychoanalytical classifications, be sure of that.

Look out at such a moment for surprises: all theories will go down with the ship when you are deciding whether to extrovert yourself in the next lifeboat, or introvert on a couple of deck chairs on your own. The first time I ever thought for myself, instead of feeling, or imagining, was when I was a bomber at the Battle of the Somme. Before then I had divided humanity into chaste and unchaste, beautiful and ugly, clever and stupid, and so forth. The biggest murder until that time in the history of war suddenly made me see that all these qualities were nothing but clothes, and I arrived with one sickening jump at the fundamental of all philosophy: that there are just two sorts of every one—those who would dig you out if you were buried alive, and the others. The givers and the takers, the fountains and the wells; and be sure you keep near the smaller class.

I wish some of all the brilliant talent that is used in examining less important or elemental differences in humanity could be applied to developing this crude truth. For I suspect that the existence, relative size and confused interaction of these two sorts of men are a lot nearer the ultimate factor of history than the superficial conflict between the "turned-outs" and the "turned-ins" of Jung, or the male and female, or even the savers for eternity and spenders of the present which all religions occupy themselves with. It may be a sort of madness that makes a certain number of people givers of themselves, their work, their lives; it certainly seems very irrational, and the most superficial experience shows that it is rare and not normal. Most of them are obviously unadjusted to life. By the very nature of things the poorer classes have a higher proportion of them than the rich. They are the "suckers." The man that actually dug me out under drum fire was a most unattractive dirty soldier, unadventurous, and slovenly. I always thought of him as something less than three-quarters witted. I don't remember his name, and have not the least idea of what happened to him; I should not be surprised if he were in jail or on the roads.

But at the same time every great man, every true artist, every genius, every "some one" is one of them too. A great business man once told me in a momentary communicativeness and indiscretion that to be really big in his own line a man had to be a bit of a sucker. I am willing to believe that; that the huckster may make a lot of money, but the heads have to be different. I know it is so in the world of books, music, art.

✦ 20 ✦

The Ductless Ideal

THE announcement of the crystallization of the female sex hormone is the latest presage and warning of the astonishing era which is almost upon us.

Here, then, is one more step toward that formidable likelihood to which the sciences of psychology and endocrinology are racing each other—the power in human hands over body and mind. As an utter layman, nothing stops me from saying right out what they only dare hint: that if this news has any meaning at all, part of it is that to all women will soon be available, at the price fixed by whatever manufacturing company gets the patent rights, beauty in a bottle. A youth-prolonger, anyway, a wrinkle-obviator, and, conditioned by a technique of use, no doubt, a potent sex-charm-increaser. . . . Only the German language really has a chance to name the marvels of our age.

87

If this particular discovery fades away, as some of the most respectably announced sometimes do in the practical developments of the laboratory, mysteriously, nevertheless it is a betting certainty that it will merely be a postponement. The doctors, trust them, are on a breast-high scent.

No doubt it would be interesting to wallow deep in speculations as to the practical uses of the finding of such an elixir, its human and also poetical results on individual and social destiny. I confess that to me personally these implications are leagues more exciting than any mere progress in mechanics.

The marvels of aeroplaning and radio are by comparison stuff for schoolboys beside this gland-magic. Here is not a question of getting to Detroit in a hurry, or whether you are going to hear "Carmen" played in London or have to whistle it yourself, but the nearing possibility of transforming the human race, body, mind and character. They are all tied up together. Why, this comes within the scope of the most inwardly important concern of the universe—poetry itself.

Even more urgent than gratitude to that noble cult or church of methodical thinkers, the scientists, on whose doings nowadays we are really more helplessly dependent than any primitives on their rain-makers, and the expression of that enormous admiration for them and their successes which any thinking man, at any rate, should feel, is a sort of duty of warning them. A warning is seldom an impertinence—ragged boys, with laths in their hands, steer the citizens off the sidewalk in Paris when they are tearing down a

88

building. It therefore implies no more than it is meant
to, if you are an arrant outsider, to warn scientists of
a certain great danger. Not of anything within their
own sphere, where their own guidance is entirely adequate, or where they themselves will change it when
necessary.

But simply that just because they have been so
successful they are nearing the brink of their own
province, and by the very force of their impetus have
started to pierce into another, where their charts,
their instruments, are worse than useless. The hazy,
misty, perilous sea of aesthetics and ethics is now in
front of them. The problem of acquiring power and
using it, or becoming rich and spending, is separate.
Having the means is separate from knowing the ideal.

That is, at a certain frontier Bacon's territory ends;
Shakespeare's begins. Beyond Einstein lies the land
of Blake. Further on than Freud you must turn to
Plato and Goethe.

This formidable necessity for an ideal is therefore
a measure of what a purely scientific method has
achieved. Fifty, twenty years ago the meaning of
good was an academic question of which science, en-
grossed in its straight course, took no heed. Professor
Huxley and Lord Kelvin had no need to worry about
the ocean of what ought to be; they were exploring the
seemingly boundless land of what is. But if Freud can
really change a character—or Jung, or Adler, or, if
you prefer, their successors—must they not have an
ideal of character as a model?

Where is that ideal? It will not suffice at all to take

it (as some of their followers and disciples at any rate sometimes appear to me to do) as fixed already, as unquestionably pre-existent. The norm to which they approach by lopping and hewing with their all-powerful tools—who fixed this?

Common sense? The very foundation of scientific method was the inexorable re-examination of everything "common sense" took for granted—the revolution of the heavens around the earth, the meaninglessness of dreams. At this supreme moment is science going to renounce its own method, and, being able to transform a man, take it for granted to what? A man without inhibitions, now that you are able to achieve him—who said that was the ideal man?

What objective induction ever arrived at this super-hypothesis: that everlasting mediocrity is mental health; that ugly plebeianism is preordained better than a little enchanting madness?

I am just as anxious about the course to be steered by the triumphant gland wizards. Having the power of beauty in their hands, masters-to-be in the inner sculpture of the body—if they should have a wrong idea of what beauty is! I cannot rid myself of the haunting dread that here, too, they will take the ideal as already settled by the first thought that comes into an ordinary man's head; that their Venus, standardly prescribed for, perhaps, will be that on the chocolate box. Just as the eugenists took, with the most scaring lack of hesitation, their Tunney ideal. How lucky it was that those, at any rate, so confident they knew what it took a Leonardo a lifetime to work out, the ideal body of a man, should not have had the power to mould humanity into it.

Furthermore, the very respect we have for these scientists, which will one day, I foresee, grow to a reverence greater than any priesthood ever enjoyed, has awkward possibilities in it. We respect so much everything they know that we are inclined to respect everything they only say. Their in sum unscientific ideals pass under cover of their scientific powers to achieve them. Here is an abyss into which you must peer, at even the risk "that at last the abyss will also gaze at thee."

✦ 21 ✦

The Coasts of Eden

A T the latest convocation of the American Philosophical Society there is a generous provision of the victuals for thought and fabric for dreams that present day science breathlessly provides us with. The bouquet of the noble display is to my fancy the promise of the gland doctors that they will soon be able to alter the stature of the human race.

The paper that announced this was a perfect symphony of the magic and folly of scientists at this point. Science to-day is like a young demiurge at the awkward age who is able to do prodigies, but has half-baked ideas on what.

91

Just why, in fact, should gland knowledge be used to increase and not decrease the size of humanity? What is there lovely or desirable not only from the aesthetic point of view, which the doctors can plead, however disingenuously, they know and care nothing about, but economically, socially generally, in eight-foot men and women? The fact is, none. The fact is they have never thought about it. And that is the flaw in their splendor that exasperates me.

For this is not an isolated case. It springs from a general and pernicious error in the scientific thought of to-day wherever its progress has been so great and practical as to bring it to the necessity for direction and ideals. In the world of Huxley, that dreary little universe that looked like a wet day in the manufacturing districts of England, without even the watery gleam of a contractual religion, ideals were not the concern of science. It was settled that nothing worth while was possible, so what might be was left to poets. Swinburne, on this, constructed his vision of a future for humanity in death, a lolling dispiritedly throughout eternity by the bank of a lukewarm water in the dark. Coney Island at midnight in August in a general strike.

But now that more enticing possibilities for humanity have arisen, strictly owing to the exquisite efforts of selfless scientists, when the sunrise of infinite possibilities has arisen, the power to fly, to change minds and now to change bodies and how many other marvels, science must provide itself with human ideals. A beggar can be indifferent to shop windows, a millionaire must learn the art of spending.

Who is this anonymous Aristotle that laid down the dimensions of desirability that science, backsliding from its principles, now takes for granted? What unknown Pope decreed that the ideal of mankind all eugenists, for example, unquestionably, unspeculatively accept, must be the progeny of a heavyweight athlete and a champion woman tennis player? They just take it for granted. What sublime exception from the sacred law of science that every assumption must be proved and tried set forth to Jung that the ideal character was a good mixer, an insensitive, society-loving man?

The same, no doubt, who sets the type all universities and schools aim for, with their complicated potent mechanisms of brain moulding, that dull-gray apotheosis of the ordinary, the centripetal herd companion, eternally tied to the apron strings of his alma mater, cold and cautious in love, squeamish in his amusements, passionately limited in his tastes as in the choice of the colors of his neckties—the college or public-school man.

And then think of those Faustian life prolongers who, sooner or later, will certainly give the world all Voronoff pretended. Who told them that the infinitely implicated power to encroach on immortality should be applied to the hinder end of life, that old age should be lengthened and not youth, that they should aim to make doddering last and not childhood?

In a hundred directions the ideal screams to be un-veiled and defined. As soon as science, with a start, realizes that the mere prejudice of the mass of commonplace humanity is no more likely to be right on humanity's ideals and interest than it was on the shape of the earth the era of discussion will be begun; the philosopher, the artist and the poet will have to be admitted in argument, with all the evidence of the literature of the past, of course, under their arms.

Believe me, they have something more to suggest than the paradise of a Wells, imitated from some charity fête of society debutantes he once witnessed from the sidewalk, or that bankrupt Quakers' meeting, which is as far as the eye of a Bernard Shaw can reach. Scientists, if you really have even the beginnings of the power over men that our Prospero possessed in his book and wand, Shelley and Shakespeare, Blake and Goya and Beethoven have something interesting to say to you.

Most urgently perhaps to these reshapers of the human form. The whole of art, treated like an incon-sequent female, in the matter which so deeply concerns it, by the gland doctors, is simply shouting a warning against the "slightly bald, somewhat larger-headed giants" it is their first astonishing aim to make. We don't want such people. If you try to transform the humanity which has a power of flowering at times into Helen of Troy, Antinous and the small-headed Her-cules in Rome into such a thing, we will destroy it as the Knights of the Round Table wiped out another, earlier evil brood of stupid monsters from the earth.

Instead of this nauseating version of the blond beast—for be sure the animal they are preparing for us is yellow-haired and weak blue-eyed (scientists prefer it)—it might seem, just offhand, that the ideal, even from the banal point of view of economics, might lie in precisely the contrary direction. Brobdingnag could only be hell for humanity long enough crucified as it has been, one would think, on the law of diminishing returns.

And the problem of crowds, that is one of the secret prime troubles of us all, would be worse with every cubic foot added to our frames. But Lilliput—that is another matter. Our present size, whoever or whatever fixed it, has always been quite out of scale with our food supply, and the six-footer was only at an advantage in a rough and tumble with wild beasts even then. But with the machine, that other mysterious and tremendous gift of science, it would immensely profit us to be pygmies.

I do not dare ask for such a size for human beings as would put them on the same wonderfully advantageous terms with our old bitterest enemy, gravity, as a beetle, which can fall from a skyscraper and pick itself up. But the size of Robin Goodfellow, say, which old Burton of the Anatomy lays down was "under two feet tall" and perfectly proportioned, would bring us back to Eden. I would make out a case for that. And if the scientists, with a dubious smile, dare to ask for the meaning of that unusual term "proportioned," I would just send him to Leonardo da Vinci, or Phidias, or the potters of Tanagra, whom long before now he ought to have consulted.

✦ 22 ✦

Dietary for Civilization

THE string end of this desperately raveled scheme of things must be education—every one knows that; and though other ages were almost as certain of it as we are, yet because it is almost the only survivor of the whole chest of hopes man used to have, religious and political, it belongs to us more distinctively even than to the Renaissance or the Greeks.

Unfortunately, in spite of the vast sums spent on it, and the respectable ability of those who spend it for us, we have not been able to get very glittering results. In most countries the product of all the schools has mainly been a socially unleavened mass of indifferent stenographers and clerks, and (of late years, with the "scientific" program) many millions of amateur automobile and radio repairers. Practically all our best men, from novelists to orangeade kings, practically all the men and women that are simply interesting and admirable, too obviously owe nothing at all to our schools and universities, either that they have resisted the system or simply escaped it altogether.

The reason for this mediocre result I believe to lie

not so much in the energy and teaching ability of our educators as in the hidden logical catches deep in the idea of education itself. Before a system of education can work there must be composed an ideal of what one hopes to produce. Most state educators are in the situation of gardeners who should dig and manure heartily without knowing if the crop is to be mushrooms or turnips. Those few systems which do undoubtedly have some ideal, like the English middle class, and some universities and Freudian baby schools, would hardly bear having it defined and discussed in the full gaze of philosophy.

Perhaps even more disastrously than this there may lurk within the idea of education some sheer practical impossibility: that as soon as you make it a communal affair it can only produce a mass product. General rules can never produce individualities; and the world is suffering from the standardization of its youths and girls.

And so every worth-while curriculum should be prefaced by the warning, "Only for individual cases." Or "Practically not transferable." An education should be an individual thing, as a tooth brush, or a wife.

With some such warning that what I propose is only intended for a small class, I want to go a little further into the question of reading for the young, which I was encouraged and astonished to find interested a large number of people, after a column on the matter of fairy tales some weeks ago. To that overwhelming majority of parents who want to use their children to satisfy their inferiority complex, who have neither confidence in their children's destiny, nor desire to make them in the least degree abnormal, individual, but of the herd, I have nothing to propose. Nor to any teachers or any schools, for the reasons I have mentioned.

But here and there, up and down the social staircase, I ask families who dream for their children a happiness outside mere conformity, those with private tutors and those with only a private shelf of books, if they have realized the importance of poetry in the fitting of children for an individual destiny, or in the training of the imagination, which is the same thing? There is a lot of miscomprehension about the matter. To try to bring up a life without ethical imagination is like trying to rear a body without vitamins—either fairy tales or religion for the babies; either poetry or religion for the later age. Very likely you can do without one, but I swear not both—or they will pay your penalty by becoming "chauffeur men," as Keyserling calls them (admiringly), just amateur taxi-drivers on the earth or in the air.

Now it is well enough, fairly well, understood that poetry is the very basis of a cultured life. It is almost as hard to acquire a taste for it in later years as is a good French accent, a knowledge of wines, or a sound set of teeth. An early musical education, I suppose, gives a sort of discipline for the emotions; a mechanical boyhood spoils you irremediably for true science. But poetry—you have to absorb that young, or you will never have an idea of what it is about.

Dietary for Civilization

There is perhaps even more misunderstanding as to how to start. The foundation, of course, is fairy tales. But even when that is complied with there are many natural pitfalls. A child, all the sort of children I am concerned with, has indeed a natural taste for poetry; and it would be safe, but not brilliant, to let them find their way themselves through a well-stocked library. Beyond that there are certain easy things to remember.

The most important, perhaps, that Shakespeare should never be imposed. He should be given in a fair, large-margined, stiff-covered edition, round about eighteen, and rather after than before. William Blake is later. His "Songs of Innocence" are not for children—how the absurd idea sprang up I can hardly imagine. Administer him, if you can, at that mystical and varying point of evolution where the soul realizes with a shudder that childhood is gone, and leans back toward it with longing and regret.

Naturally avoid all baby poems, for the same reason. He or she should have his "Mother Goose" by heart. But these are not baby poems. They are tatters of archaic, and often even only eighteenth century, satire and sophistication. I think many do not understand that Longfellow (not, for heaven's sake, Whittier at all), Bryant and even Joaquin Miller are not dead poets. Such are excellent for children. Many a pure taste has been awakened by "Olaf" and the "Tales of a Wayside Inn"; they have an age limit to them.

Another treasure, unjustly misesteemed because it

99

is not realized that what is good for boyhood is not for adolescence, is the narrative poems of the heroic time. I particularly suggest instead of some misleading insipidity about aviators—there is a sort of boys' book infinitely more corrupting to the imagination than Nick Carter—the "Lara," "Corsair," "Mazeppa" series of Byron. Yes, Byron. And at ten is the time for the "Idylls of the King." For Coleridge, who, however, will last through life. Not for Wordsworth. At the marvelous season of seventeen, the spring of the heart, then a soul, so opened should be ready to take in with ecstasy the great lyrics, careering, like a canoe on the rapids, toward the great waterfalls: Shakespeare, the Elizabethans, the precipice of "Hamlet," "Romeo," "Othello," "Lear," "Paradise Lost."

✦ 23 ✦

Radio

OUR age, which is cursed with inhuman savagery and want, also allows us superhuman pleasures. The most terrific of all our compensations for living in these days is this unnatural power of "listening in." Its enjoyment is as general as taxes; like so significant a number of our modern inventions, its benefits go as far as the limits of the race, and have no partiality for a class. The workman, the clerk, whose means so seldom extend to a first class cinema, still less to those rare and expensive occasions when a real singer is singing real music, are the very favorites of the marvel.

The great inventors and scientists, like the greatest business men, are often universal benefactors beside whom the most renowned saints of religion cut a poor figure. The glorious perfecter of Radio has done more in a year for drab millions the world over than all the amiable missionaries of the nineteenth century together.

His mark is the antenna wire, which for countless miles of hopeless backdoors is hung out to mark that there lives one who has broken through loneliness, conquered poverty and forgotten misery in possession of a pragmatical secret that was out of reach even of the dreams of ancient magicians. This wire that slants or sags from millions of chimney pots to forlorn trees, or the biscuit-tin roofs of chicken sheds, or simply to the copings of soot-rooted walls, ties its owner to the life of the whole world, from which he seemed endlessly separated; and by the most immediate and living of senses, not cold sight but human and familiar hearing.

So night after night dumb millions fiddle with knobs and hear with ravishment, as if they were behind a thin door, the voices of the supreme culture of their times. And over backs of countless dreary houses are strung like metallic spider webs these ennobling wires; a new and graceful ornament to the somewhat infernal architecture of our times.

Even in my remote village in France one can share

in the bonus which science has given mankind. Here, too, all the voices of all the world come nightly. With a twirl of a vulcanite wheel, as delicately engraved as a leaf under a microscope, one hears every nation in turn. At a neatly ruled distance of millimetres from the scratching, droning call of Paris is London herself; Daventry, Frankfurt, Barcelona, Rome. After our midnight, instantaneously across an infinite waste of waves, is America.

Sometimes tumbling upon each other in the whole gambit are a dozen great nations to be overheard, in full practice of their separate cultures, to decide whose relative values we fought four years. As yet the army of small talents and great tacts, who rush joyfully on any possibility of the one new career we have invented, National Propaganda, have for some reason missed the Radio; so for a time the listener can hear undoctored truth about the rival cultures. Daventry talks to Englishmen, as yet oblivious that under the eaves are millions of foreigners to be impressed, and patriotically deceived on the education and culture that the nation enjoys; and so with all the rest.

Perhaps all these states soon will realize that strangers are watching them in their intimate amusements, and will begin to show off. Perhaps until directional wireless comes they will have to continue in their naïveté, for all propaganda must have two versions, and the home folk might not care to sacrifice their amusement for an impression to be made abroad.

To-day, then, the wireless is indiscreet. Berlin can

hear, almost blushing, the clumsy and unpoetic rubbish of London's "Children's Hour." Rome can hear the chant, which lasts for hours, of Paris Bourse prices, for which the Frenchman, like the fabulous miner with his bathroom, meanly uses an exquisite luxury. The squalls of the tenors who never leave Rome clash and "interfere" with the maudlin waltzes that Hamburg really hums.

The Radio unites Europe in more than one respect. Most of all in the evening, when each nation sends through limpid ether the flower of art which gives civilization meaning, and by which each would agree to be judged in the light of eternity. And then from one after the other spins the little superheterodyne over all its half-circles of selectivity; from England, Spain, Italy, Germany and France, comes with gracelessly cheerful monotony the rhythmic chirping of an American jazz.

Each nation doubtless has contributed something to the immense sum of ingenuity and knowledge which led to this machine; but when the doors are shut, and they are in family in their shirt sleeves, they have found nothing of their own: they play the same tunes. There seems something almost dishonorable in the wireless when you make this discovery, something of prying into intimacy that should be respected; but along with this feeling you may be inclined (if only the trumpet worked backward) to shout jovially, with a distant chuckle to old and ripe-cultured Europe, whose propagandists have almost come to deceive

themselves, "So this is Europe when you are by yourselves."

✦ 24 ✦

Artist of the Poor

THEY often find Cretan pots in the royal ash-
heaps of Egypt which are photographed in colors
in great subsidized folios; one little shard is enough to
make a university digger's reputation. But no one for
hundreds of years will write about the visible traces
of another great civilization that is exporting artist
work to every arc of the earth in our days; no doubt
the only reflections of old Egypt's sociologists—before
they were mummied—on this Cretan ware were that
home production of faïence was scandalously in need
of protection.

Where, except in the privately printed essays of
small Chelsea personalities out to shock the world into
recalling their names or in the villainous propaganda
of professional advertisers, will you find any reference
to-day to a certain sort of wares, not sparsely dissemi-
nated in rare examples in palaces, precious but very
small, like the beads the Phoenicians traded to Britain,
or the vases with the octopus motive that they find at
Thebes—but huge and human works of art with which
in our days the minds of millions are being delighted

104

and their innermost motives bent to match a different
way of life: the American film?

This is the most obvious cultural factor in Europe
to-day; there is not a hamlet between the Atlantic and
the Soviets in which it is not nightly in play.

In a remote working suburb of Florence where I
strayed one Saturday afternoon there was a crude
sign propped up almost in the last street. Around it
there was a larger and more intent crowd than I had
seen in the central square in front of the latest procla-
mation of the dictator; it was a notice that a year-old
edition of a film by the Gish sisters had at last arrived
at this corner of the earth. From there it would go
deeper still into the branch-line geography of Italy—
and when at last, blurred and yellowed, it had been
seen by every housewife in the Italian back country,
it would go on to Tunis, or Tripoli, and even then its
strangest adventures would have only begun.

Even paper money does not circulate so far as the
film. And these things are not condensed formulas,
mere ejaculations of beauty that are all the mightiest
ceramist could compress into his ware, but long state-
ments, encouragements, explanations—complete and
widespread works of art which have not only a circulation immeasurably wider than the most universal
books that have ever been printed (Charles Chaplin
is famous in hinterlands where they have never heard
of the Bible), but also because they possess both the
power of the picture and the power of the story, a
vastly more intimate influence.

Wherever there is a light—or a hall—these artists of America are in contact with humanity, which to its confines is their public. You might find thirty years ago, behind an open window in a rickety skyscraping tenement in Marseilles or Moscow, a girl spelling by lamp-light a worn edition of "Les Miserables," or even "L'Assommoir." But in these cases of an incredible diffusion of influence the reader would be an exception—a concierge's studious daughter, a self-improving workman; at any rate, one who could read.

But Charlie makes Chinese laborers laugh, and Kaffirs in the compounds of the Rand; he and his peers alone of all the artists that have ever existed have outgrown selectivity of audience.

Chaplin is the artist of the poor; perhaps the first who has ever existed. He is the living legend of the proletariat, which his wry, Quixotic smile, his pariah rags, his lamentable feet, express. Where else but under the weight of what modern industrialism has put on suffering humanity could any feet have been flattened and distorted as his? For what savages except the slaves of the machine ever have been condemned to wear such trousers?

With these visible and too recognizable badges of the men at the base of things, by the same genius he has invented for himself a parable into which each of his appearances are only continuations and episodes —a sort of proletarian Don Quixote, as deep as it is passionately interesting, in which he merges all the ramifications of the protest of the under-dog—the an-

cient cycle of the slave, the folklore of Bre'r Rabbit,
the revenge of the humble.

✦ 25 ✦

Poor Jews

POVERTY is harder to bear in the United States
than in Europe. This is the structural truth, like
a skeleton, covered with the living flesh of episode,
description, character development, that gives Michael
Gold's "Jews Without Money," form and strength. It
is also an aspect of what I believe to be the only true
and elementary psychological differentia of America.
The thousands of other differences that thousands of
foreign and native observers have claimed to find I
believe either accidental or founded on a malcompari-
son. Thus Siegfried of Strassburg says that Americans are essentially religious even to superstition. But
every year nearly a million of his logical and sceptical
Frenchmen go to Lourdes on Pilgrimage. Sinclair
Lewis in his earlier period was always implying, that
rural and provincial life in Europe is not mean, petti-
fogging and ignorant, as it is, they say, here. But
Main Street is a world thoroughfare. It runs through
every small town in Italy, France, Germany—for all
I know, through the most remotely mysterious provinces of inner China.

Class for class, individual for individual, setting

107

peasant against peasant, clerk against clerk (and not, as the gravest Europeans are so fond of doing, comparing their own élite with an American majority), there is only one difference that resists analysis. It is nothing to do with baths, or literary taste, or dress, or manner. You will find the most unpleasant "Americanism" not over here, but among the bull-necked business men of Berlin. The fiercest dollar chasing, the greatest speed of business life, is around the Place de la Bourse in Paris and not in Wall Street. With every difference but one you can find, more or less ingeniously, its finest expression somewhere over the Atlantic. But underneath them all, giving their whole a reality, which singly cannot stand, is this, that the whole of American life is dominated by the hope of becoming rich.

That is the other side of Mr. Gold's thesis. His Jews (and his scale is big enough to include the whole vast squirming mass of the newly arrived immigrants) find ultimately, as the father in the book puts it, "It is better to be dead in this country than not to have money." A hope, if it is big enough, can poison a life much more thoroughly than most despairs, for hope is more essentially an irritant than a soporific. So this fundamental hope of America, that eternally insistent possibility of riches, fortune, power, refuses to allow these poor millions to do as they did even in the worst circumstances at home: develop a philosophy, lie in the sun, and snuggle together when it is snowing. They can never adapt themselves, as they did in the Ghetto, to far worse externals, grow a technique of poverty, as it

were. The tyranny of the hope of riches nags them
night and day worse than their fleas.

Only one main character in his book escapes the
spell that makes the rest misers, gangsters, hypochon-
driacs, and that is "mother." In one vital quality, that
I would have to search far and wide in my memory to
find equaled, his portrait of this woman is magnificent.
How rare indeed it is to find a character in a modern
novel whose ideas of right and wrong are sound; who
behaves, as it were, artistically; for ethics is a sort of
art, and behavior can be beautiful or ugly. This Jewish mother has a sense, let us say, of honor which would
not disgrace the heroes of Conrad, far removed from
the dirty, stupid little ways. I saw a play the other
night in which the audience was asked to admire (and
did) a wife wriggling out of a divorce disaster by the
most terrible meannesses, lying, "framing" a poor
devil of a detective, cheating all round as if she was
wielding a broadsword in the Highland manner.

But Mr. Gold in this book has given us a noble
woman, not some common mixture of virago, cheat
and harpy. Perhaps in the whole work, which is
crowded with unforgettable pictures of reality, it is
this that is best. Alone of them all, she has kept her
head and steers until the book itself, with its whole
cargo, comes safe into port. It is she, the poor Jewish
mother, who with really exquisite precision of feeling
refuses the thousand dollars indemnity for her little
girl's death from the truck owners, yet accepts
cheerfully a five-dollar present from a kindly prosti-
tute.

"But don't tell your poppa," she said. "He is too proud."

I love that woman, and Socrates would have loved her. At last in a naturalist novel we have some one who is not canaille, some one utterly unvulgar.

On this cornerstone, and endowed with the solid framework I started to talk about, the whole work stands up, something quite different from mere propaganda or the mere cataloguing of woes and disasters that so often masquerade as "pictures of real life." It is as solid and complete as a thesis, four-sided like a building.

The whole Jewish east side is there, not a mere trick photograph intended to startle and surprise you. Not a scent has been forgotten, hardly a sound of the rushing confusion of this latest, perhaps most curious, adventure of that race which has experienced and shared in every major experience of humanity since the building of the Pyramids. The hot nights on the roofs, the sight of gangsters' pigeons wheeling in the ineffably blue New York sky, the children prospecting the ash cans, the expeditions to Heber's Cheap Store; infinite curiosities, pains and pleasures of childhood on the east side. Of course Mr. Gold is a communist. He himself has gone on into what probably in the future, as the riches hope fades from America in the next century, will be its substitute as divine irritant in the lives of the poor—the social hope. The revolution —well, well. His "mother" would probably think this too, when pushed beyond the sensible firmness against oppression she always rightly displayed, almost as

110

noxious and destructive of the real business of life as the other. I suppose she would be wrong, and humanity must not be allowed to settle down and just live. But I share her hankering. "What do you want? Bread enough. A roof. Healthy children. What more?"

✦ 26 ✦

The Celestial Sausage

I SAW the Graf Zeppelin pass north that night on its voyage home. From the little attic window on that side of the house you can see the tower and the statue of the Papal Palace of Avignon on a clear day or night. At about half past ten the moon, half grown, was already a certain number of degrees on its ascent. The night was entirely quiet except for the frogs, the crickets and the nightingales, who were executing their exciting play symphony. The noise of the machine came across dull and stealthy, which attracted the attention first of one of the servants, who called up the whole house to see the monster, progressing unfluctuatingly, about six miles away.

This enemy would be the terrible mistral, the implacable wind of Provence, that comes like a river of air flowing parallel to but above the Rhone, along the same grand route from the Alps to the Mediterranean Sea. This wind, I believe, is as old as the river. In the middle ages they used to curse it as they do to-day. And the Avignon people were just as ruefully proud of it. If you give them time enough, men will boast and be sentimental about anything that afflicts them specially and marks them out. So all the peasants of the region, from Ventoux to Marseilles, had a sort of pleasure—one of those mean, human pleasures— when the Zeppelin was caught and nearly destroyed by this pestilential mistral as Eckener tried disastrously to get back against it from Spain.

Since even the grandiose gales of the Atlantic could not do as much, the mistral must be without a rival in the champion forces of nature, and that pleases its local victims, as if they owned it. It is a desiccative, nervous wind at all times, so frequent that all the trees for a hundred square miles grow leaning at 80 degrees to the ground—cypresses and even olive trees. When it is really exasperated, as Eckener found it in his first experience, it makes a noise in all the trees like that the waves make against a breakwater; and in gusts for hours at a time it is just as if we were in a chasm in the air which the whole atmosphere of Europe was rushing in to fill up.

The Zeppelin had no chance against this aerial tide. Airplanes can cut into it without much difficulty, but this huge spinner's shuttle had no chance. The wind and the sea can be fought only by slashing, not by pushing. The fight lasted a whole day and a night; four engines out of five were smashed; most of the time the unlucky adventurers on board were as sick as cats with that final abomination, air-sickness.

The world has disinterest enough nowadays to find

something pathetic about German hopes, that undis-courageable striving to beat the rest of mankind which has substituted the Zeppelin for whatever they were once trying to do with their army.

For their poetical and obsessed belief in dirigibles is something quite out of proportion to practical affairs. The extreme possibilities of this means of transport are not sufficient grounds for the rapt enthusiasm of the whole nation on each essay of it, the awe-struck attention with which they watch hourly its vicissitudes. If a whole fleet of Zeppelins were in regular, and even economic, operation across the Atlantic, and across the great land mass of the Old World; if, as they seem sincerely to believe, there is a possibility of such a traffic, still the emotion is out of all measure.

Germany invented the Zeppelin. It is that vanity, that patriotism, which is why the makers of these curious monsters, so disappointing in their development, so visibly unlikely to be a practical solution, find capital untiringly at their service; why no accident, no catastrophe, will stop their progressive manufacture. These Germans have developed the use of the airplane as high as any other state at least. But their interest in that is tepid, businesslike and sober, because it is an invention from America. Zeppelinism is a national cult.

For that reason it has its mythology. Its commander, as we remember from the incidents of his last successful voyage to New York, behaves like a haughty high priest. There is an atmosphere of sacred secrecy, even about its technique, wholly unscientific, which the

113

Germans themselves not only admit but are proud of. None but navigators will ever be able to steer these hippogriffs. They obey secret words which are not included in their sale price.

And, as is customary in mystical undertakings, there is a subsidiary art, as Socrates would call it, of finding explanations—romantic, dramatic explanations—for all the connected mishaps. Passengers are sworn to secrecy before they embark. If an engine, let alone four, breaks down in the roaring war with the wind, it is that the hidden hand is at work. A humane rescue, such as the meanest Levantine fisherman caught in a storm would expect and receive as a natural right, when it happens to the Zeppelin is magnified to a turning point in international affairs. That the French sailors tow the beaten leviathan into a shed at Toulon proves that peace with France is possible; one great Berlin paper said that it would forever alter the feeling between the two nations. Another thought the occasion came to alter the whole code of fortified places in the world, so that another Zeppelin could demand to fall into a foreign fort as a right.

So the shadowy look was not altogether the effect of moonlight and the dark, sleeping landscape that night. The Zeppelin is a collective reverie, very likely the only one of that bursting magazine of dreams and phantasies in the head of Germany to survive the war. Whatever happens to it materially, whatever smash or failure, will be repaired by fathomless resources of the will to believe.

And, as in the case of individuals, nations and states are never so human (that peculiar quality made up of pathos and the grotesque) as in their dreams. This supreme figment, this desperately loved ambition of the desperately human Germany, has a resemblance which others than cynics and mockers can observe to a missile thrown into the wind, or, still more curiously, to an immense flying sausage, a frankfurter in the sky.

✦ 27 ✦

The Science of Stamps

INLAID here and there between the plate-glass fronts of the antiquity shops in every rich city in Europe are more sober strips of window-dressing, usually not more than a door and a pane—the stamp dealers. Separating these are romantic jumbles of old and curious porcelain, rosewood, lace, ivory and gold, the general heritage of Europe's past, in which every tourist is attracted to buy a share.

These stamp dealers make a more austere and unintelligible display. The antiquary's shelves show off his baubles where chance has set them. But behind his small neighbor's windows are the invisible bones of a system. No untidy art, but a pretty science governs the philatelist's rows of tiny colored rectangles and adjusts their transparent gum hinges on the card-

115

board, numbered strips and albums that exactly fit his window, in a soft-colored mosaic as prim as Queen Victoria's bedspread.

At most, the dealer in these precious scraps allows a fat envelope or two of bargains to hang from clips on a horizontal string to break the order. To every fish its own bait. Any one can like the cut glass of Queen Anne, or the clay fairies of Dresden. Stamp collecting is an esoteric business. It is a Puritan in our Vanity Fair; it strictly abjures all poetries and vulgar utilities. Here they deal only in the very essence of rarity.

By this fanaticism, philately has universally spread; by this mark it is no mere hobby. Philately is a characteristic of modern culture. It is the unique refinement of our civilization. All other vices, all other tastes we have inherited from an ancestor age that excelled us in them. The passion for treasuring used postage stamps we ourselves invented.

The sole customers of the stamp shops, wherever you may find them, are from the two socially supreme classes of our age: schoolboys, the propagators of sport; millionaires, the corner stones of capitalism. They never conflict in their purchases. The fat envelopes are for the boys; the single lonely specimens for the rich men. Without millionaires stamp collecting would languish; without schoolboys it would never have existed. They are both necessary; and from their interplay in the cult rays shoot on the secret places of our inextricable times.

Stamp collecting is a chapter in sociology. It began

in the '50s, naturally in England, for that first sufferer from the mechanical revolution set the ways of life for the whole world besides. It was a by-product of the self-improvement tide, which has not spent itself today. These '50s were the days of spelling bees, and serial educators, and popular zoology, when the miserable multitudes, under the fierce incitements of Samuel Smiles, flung themselves into the desks of Faraday, Sir Robert Ball and Rev. H. Wood to get some cure for their economics in the "systematic acquirement of scientific knowledge."

Science was tipsy with logic, and reeled after Linnaeus's old dream of a straight classification of all living things: easy, complete. Science is the way out of the 16-hour day, hoped the clerks and ambitious workmen, and science is simply card-indexing. Thousands of natural history books with six plates in litho at three and sixpence preached the way to get on by counting and alphabeting the stamens of wild flowers.

When the bubble burst, under the uncountable variety of creation, it left an heir in this game. Since beetles and sea-urchins and the wonders of the microscope refuse to have a grammar of size and shape, let us find a field of knowledge more manageable, where every example can be distinguished by rule, where every rare exception may be known. The disappointed amateur scientists, with the satisfying smack of the ruined taste for learning in their mouths, looked around and saw the schoolboys playing with a science game.

Camera Obscura

Those colored tabs of adhesive paper the Government sold as receipts for postage, so convenient in size, so cheap, so varied; so amenable to reason and classification. Schoolboys who collect all the activities of man, once they can get rid of the contaminating ethics, had long discovered philately. So, a new hobby appeared.

The first error roofed its success. Some poor employee in a fright found out he had printed the Queen's head upside down on a batch of stamps. Those which had been sold were "errors," precious exceptions, which every science (so much they had learned) must have. Stamp collecting followed the Bible, and cloth caps, and calico, and football and all the vast apparatus of steam culture round the world. It grew and flourished wherever the railways ran and wherever they cut up companies into joint stock.

The number of its separate pieces became like the stars; it had to be divided, even for the most encyclopaedic collector, into countries; but each of these countries remained definite and complete, knowable to its last watermark and perforation. Men who had played with it to beguile the time grew rich, and continued adepts to the mock-science. They brought back a little of the ethical smear the boys had wiped off; excused themselves to miscreants by holding, "It teaches geography."

They hoarded the errors and varieties which had once puzzled their albums, as things without price, and trafficked them with their fellows for the price of coun-

The Science of Stamps

try parks. And when the war came philately was ready for its last charge.

Until then there were high prices, but they were paid by lovers of the game. Suddenly into the auction rooms, where the peaceful sect of stamp fanciers are outbidding each other, modestly rushes the rabble, the investing rabble from the picture rooms, who do not want to learn geography in the least, who do not even pretend to admire the faded pastel colors of a Mauritius Blue, but have come, as they came to Titian sales, to buy at any price to hoard or sell again.

Two post-war horrors drove them: revolution and death dues. A Grand Duke at the frontier would be stripped to the buff and shot if he was wearing his wife's pearls. But an honest stamp-collecting million-aire could get through any sentry with an old envelope in his pouch on which stuck a used stamp sufficient to keep him in three meals for life in any exile.

The fame of this spread in days when all property seemed desperately unportable. Death would not dry up the benefits of such an investment. What can the super-tax collector say to a dying multi-millionaire who passes, hand to hand, to his favorite heir a little envelope with 50 prime errors; a little fortune that never will pay tax? Saved from the death dues, that, at any rate.

Its birth in a schoolboy game, its growth to a private currency among world millionaires: these are phenom-ena fantastic even in our peculiar age.

The Pope's Own Scrap-Book

IT takes many thousands of utterly different lives to make a Capital. Their interesting diversity, not their wealth, or culture, lifts such cities from mere provincial settlements. By this essence Rome is equal to Paris or London. It is hard to get a book here, there are no manufactures; the women are dowds compared with those of Milan or flashy Turin, and uglier besides; but the vast variety of employments saves it from provincialism. Here are Kings, Bootboys, Tyrants, Spadassins, Profiteers, and Lyric Poets. On each man's trade hangs the tune of the life of his dependents; these in turn interplay in circles on another, till the diversity propagates itself in open results in the public streets and squares. Because they all earn their living in different ways, the Roman crown is un-uniform in its clothes, in its walk, in its tastes, above all, in its faces. And in such a city the queer tag-ends of stories into which every loiterer has a chance of falling at street corners, and all those unsubstantial interesting incidents, deliciously incomplete, which men call "adventures," have an immensely increased likelihood. Every day I walk in Rome one of these minute bright results of the clash of innumerable differences, like electric sparks jumps out and startles me. Once I heard a dwarf three feet high yelling in a profound bass voice at a pretty trollop in a night alley. Once

The Pope's Own Scrap-Book

I saw, at a newspaper kiosk, a client wait while the owner with a pretence of indifference stuffed a paper in his pocket without a word—the circulation of censored news. Twice I have leaped with a curse out of the way of a magnificent moving automobile and looked in the window as it passed—to see the unforgettable melodramatic mask of the Duke himself: Mussolini on his way to a council of state. Rome is a real capital.

It has the supreme distinction of not only being wonderfully different in its parts, in the hundreds of thousands of personalities its walls enclose, but it excels and differs from all the rest of European Capitals in one whole side of its life. It has the Vatican and the Papal Court; which is more remarkable than all other courts. At Buckingham Palace I am sure I should see, as I have seen at great political receptions in London, a huge homogeneous crowd of noble replicas, all healthy, sun-browned, tall, all talking on the same note of the same bets and games, of the same lives in the open air. In Paris, at the Elysée no one can forget the horde of politicians and industrials, like a regiment in a uniform of fur collars and unworthy boots; all preoccupied with a good place at the buffet at eleven o'clock.

But in Rome, at the Vatican, there is more than the pomp of kings, more story and life; and after all (though one must not be too particular nowadays), more weighty importance behind the whispered conversations, the presentations, the antechambers, and the alcoves, than in any President's birthday party in France. The Pope still has the most secure power of any individual in the world. It adds a savor to his great receptions which some palates need before they can enjoy such shows, like mustard with roast beef.

But it is not the policy and the power, the grave intrigues and decisions, that one feels behind every curtain; settling what education Uraguayan children are going to have for the next generation, or altering the speed of the Westernization of China, about which I know nothing at all, that interested me when I saw the Pope in his court, but the costumes, the diversities of color and costume and shape, set like a picture in ancient luxury. And especially that rich and entrancing collection of human faces. Not in the whole world can be seen in a single element of space such an extraordinary show of what not only distinguishes our cardinal mystery, our separate personalities from each other, but displays like a revealed diary, our education, our life, our sorrows, our ambitions, our blood, our adventures, the human countenance. There is the natural Roman diversity, the immense range of silhouette and expression of a very old individualist race, the Roman patricians. There are the greater differences of race and climate in this throng of prelates from all parts of the world, white, black, red, yellow, with the troubling varieties that the Latin races have created in the Americas. The eye may bend from the good, stupid mustachios of a giant Swiss Guard to the mysterious, withheld sentimentality of a Chinese Bishop. In common crowds the philosophic onlooker may be content indeed if he can unparcel the broad classes by race: say such is an Indian, such an American on holiday from the Middle West, and get enough amusement from the guessing game. But here one is irresistibly launched into more subtle conjecture; into surmise about character, brain force, history, and can even taste greedily the rare joys of the pure collector. Not a few of these spiritual potentates come from the earth's ends on mission here have that most unusual possession, for which in general we have to be content to pore over the treasures of the great painters, Velasquez, Rembrandt, Holbein—an absolutely unusual face. Even now the physiognomist's privilege is not completed. Here is no uncatalogued, haphazard jumble of rarities set out without order, in a monotony which baffles the eye, but (by the accident of history) the Pope's court is not only the most complete on earth, but it is enhanced by the finest, the most revealing aids of costume. It may be that a Rotary Club dinner could assemble an almost equal display of grave, dignified, imposing men. But without costume the admirable light-purple of the cardinals, this red-yellow-blue of the Guards, these caps, tonsures, cockades, these mitres, stoles, rochets, cassocks, these silks and lawns and unparalleled damasks and velvets, they would be outshone without comparison. You can see the difference, even from where I stood as the Pope entered to give audience, in a humble corner yards away, that perfect costume can make to the full revelation of the human face.

It was in a side chancel of the Museum. On each side of the arm down which they passed were the statues of the Roman emperors. On marble corbels between were the busts of their wives and courtiers. Octavius Cæsar held up a gray finger toward the Pope's throne in admonition. A satyr sniggered down at my feet, as irrelevant to this assembly of great ones as myself and the pimpled seminarist at my side. It seemed, now they were all ranged together, these strong-jawed Romans, that all their men looked Irish, and all their wives like English matrons. These long-dead heathens had not the complete variety of the living Christians that moved among them. What faces of venerable Cardinals—romantic, ascetic, ambitious princes of this Church. Hawks, Doves, even a Bull among them; faces of living ivory, wax, iron, scarred and inscribed with the unmistakable records of long lives of the brain and the heart. How different the Pope from them all, as striking as the most marvelous of them, but with a look of another sort: in his immaculate satin the very type not of a visionary hermit, but of a shrewd, courteous old American banker.

But when the eye unwillingly left the ecclesiastics and wandered to the ranges of the Noble Guard on service it was like looking into a folio illustrated Lavater. Here for a portrait painter were all possible types, from thin, vaporous dreamers to untimely Bonapartes. One of them, I remember, possessed a characteristic which I have never before seen—instead of curving up and out over his bulging blue eyes, this unknown Noble had his black, long eyelashes turned down and inward. Hapsburg chins, Bourbon noses, all the famous birth signs and tares of Europe's aristocracy set in order round the gold dais. I stared long and earnestly, be sure, at this anthology of faces, a treasure for the painter, for the novelist, for drama; where, perhaps for the first time, a reverent spectator could conceive the enormous, fascinating diversity of the human individual, the essence of life's adventure and interest, the secret of a capital city—at the Pope's Court, in the Jubilee Year, in Rome.

✦ 29 ✦

Coliseum: a Coffin

ROME— The grandeur of this city still serves indifferently as an advertising pretext for many important state theories: Colonial expansion, Anglo-Saxon imperialism and the Fascist press censorship. Its highest visible symbol, they say, is the Coliseum: at night, under a full moon, preferably, as Goethe, Byron, Hugo saw it. So to-night I persuaded a Roman hackney driver to take me there after dinner. Even the most stiff-necked hater of sights falters when he is within a mile of the Coliseum, if only worried with curiosity to see if innumerable others have said the truth. In twenty minutes from the river bank where I had meaninglessly strayed, his poor beast stumbled up a last hill, a long grassy incline striped with eight tram lines, and over the edge I saw my goal.

It fills a deep hollow down to which the pent slants

125

with three hair-pin bends. Even so the descent is rapid. The municipality has put up flimsy pine railings painted white for the safety of night traffic. I do not know if this last hill has always existed or if it has grown through 2,000 years by the natural attrition of human works and buildings, like a kitchen midden. Along the last level are many gnawed sections of brick-work, like the débris of a wedding cake, by the side of the road. On the other side is the Tower.

A circle such as this in the obscurity keeps an un-weakened impression of immensity, of boundless size which square walls cannot attain. The geometry of this Coliseum aided by the night makes it seem greater than a mountain. The eye is not lost in any irregular peaks and shoulders, but it recognizes the circle. All that Europe has kept from a lesser past, the Gothic ranges, the Renaissance hills of masonry, is impressively worn and eaten by time, but the Coliseum has been used dif-ferently. Its stupendous piers have not suffered pa-tiently like younger things. Time has splintered them, has smashed their solid stone, gnashed great bites out of them, as if by explosion. Its wear has left sharp edges, and the fragments which have fallen to the ground are angular. It seems dangerous to pass through these cavernous entrances. Inside every foot of ground is littered with ruined brickwork and fallen blocks of stone, past which are irregular fragments of the fine blue of the night sky. Through ragged holes in the rock above glimmer phases of the same light.

In the centre, these caves open into a topless cage. Barring you from all but the zenith of the sky is an immense mesh of stonework. The empty apertures have no human semblance to doors or arches. They are plainly parts of the mechanism of a trap. Silhouetted against one of them is something, not a fallen length of corbel, not an ancient lintel, I swear but a giant's head and shoulders as big as a church, attentive and silent. A strip of coarse grass is underfoot, and further on still, an iron grating round some monstrous excavation that blocks escape to the free centre, where once gladiators fought in the sand. African beasts, tigers from India, wild boars from the Thuringian forests were once housed there, like monster rats in these deserted holes.

There is an unmeasured air of fatigue over the whole place, the waiting silence of despair of an antiquity that cannot escape. Only from outside steal in, very comforting, single, inconsequent hoots of a taxicab, the rattle and jar of a tramcar descending the hill with a crammed freight of tired Roman shop girls, for they close late. My cab, too, is waiting.

On the top of the hill, the driver breathes his pitiable horse. The round bulk below now lies in another aspect. There are electric lights, I notice, strung round it on steel posts, each of two weak lamps, inside a grid of wire. The Coliseum seems more proportionate now that the whole sweep of the sky is visible. Over it all, the immortal giant Orion, his glittering belt rising perpendicular to a great crack in the coping, and the dim group of the Pleiades. Eternally young, they triumph in the firmament over the weatherworn body of the giant figuration of human grandeur and world conquest below. This, then, is the Coliseum, symbol of old Rome, which in a mystery fires the imagination of rulers still to bad emulation of its makers. Sinister, villainous, unutterably melancholy, it lies there fallen under the mocking serenity of the sky, sullen, huge witness of the stupidity of power, the mortality of all empire; not a throne or a shrine, but a huge round, indestructible stone coffin.

✦ 30 ✦

Foch Goes to Notre Dame

MARSHAL FOCH had two elevations, like a corner block building. In his blue service uniform, with the stars on his sleeve, as we used to see him bustling up or down the steps of entrance to the great hotels which housed the peace delegations in Paris, he had the aura of pre-eminence that makes men feel young and small as well as respectful, like schoolboys or freshmen. The hand had a reflex jerk to the cap, even in great financiers, and foreign Generals and politicians, who are almost as much afraid to be deferential as they, often must have found it hard to resist the instinctive motion of the fingers to cover the lighted end of the cigars in the hollow of the hand.

Such was the distinctive prestige of the Marshal's appearance: something of the headmaster, something of the grandfather, something, in fact, of the constitutional King—he was the sort of leader who has to take pains to soften his natural authority and not, which is more common, to cultivate it. A certain amount of the grotesque perfects such a presence, as a slight stammer does a wit. Foch was deplorably bandy, and for the obvious queer human reasons that would be so hard to put into words this kept off any resentment even from the vainest of those who stood aside or rose up at his passage.

In the saddle, of course, this vanished, as if he put it away with his pipe to go on parade. The sight of him, which I had, riding through the Arc de Triomphe with his starry baton in his hand at the head of Victory was the essential expression of military glory, exempt from the slightest staginess or self-consciousness which, luckily, for the sake of its effects on the imagination of the young, never can be adequately expressed in art. The shams of war have been enough betrayed for me to admit that Foch on his charger was as noble, as poised, as sublime as a Bengal tiger in liberty, and made the fact clear, usually hidden by our biped ridiculousness, that man is, after all, the lord of creation.

As such he was one of the faces of humanity. But in civilian clothes, with a derby hat, it was not so good. He was no longer the Olympian schoolmaster, but a mere professor, underpaid and learned, the sort of respectability the best of us have a sneaking unworthy contempt for. The human male may be divided sartorially (which means, I suppose, erotically, though that is a queer idea) into those who look best in uniform, and those, an infinite minority, who don't. Foch belonged emphatically to the former, like most Latins —which has its own deep, implicated history.

The one quality common to his two appearances was real. He was a cultured man—there were many regions of civilized thought and expression where he was disinclined to venture, but not any capital cities. He had some Greek and Latin, and used them. Certainly history was his chosen walk, but, excluding the gases and clouds, he was well nourished all his life with all the solids of world literature, provided they were not anti-Christian and were translated into French. Such men pile up evidence for the revolt that is due in another ten or twelve years against specialization for the highest ambitions.

With all this he was above all a logician, a virtuoso in logic. His canonical life motto, whatever he may have said as his last words, the phrase they will teach to St. Cyr neophytes for a hundred years to come, was "De quoi s'agit-il?" (What's the matter?), which is the incomparable tool logic supplies for tackling any problem whatever. As for his technical art, I, who never could read the first line of strategy, have heard it said by connoisseurs that he handled armies like a hydraulic engineer. That sounds plausible, for I discovered for myself that men in the mass are just a sticky liquid with the special property of flowing uphill.

The problem of Foch is how on earth such a dreary, brain-destroying way of life as the military career could produce such a first class, tempered intelligence. Every one knows or suspects the ordinary grind of a garrison life through which an officer has to pass, until his old age, his advancement and a war coincide to give him a use. The jealousies of the wives, the mean snobbery which infests all "gentlemen's professions," the awful round of a social life which rarely has money in its veins. To this must be added for the French officer both the eternal alertness in mess room intrigue necessary for advancement, and the politico-religious situation.

The French pre-war officer had to be a keen churchman and reactionary to please his Generals, and he had a fanatically anti-clerical Government behind them. Foch went so far as to have a distinguished Jesuit for a brother, the equivalent under the French radical Government of looking for a political career in Georgia with a touch of colored blood. Yet he survived and emerged. The highest part of the art of life is the expectation of miracles.

The days of the romantic splendors and miseries of a military life are over. Very likely Foch himself thought of his conquest of Ludendorff, the half-Wallenstein, as allegorical. Foch and the new Generals are not romantic; it is the staid boy and not the young Bonapartes who will love the model. When Foch was still young, Déroulède could not get a single officer to help him in his coup d'état, not even Marchand of Fashoda, and got the famous blow with the flat of the sword for trying to.

There was no adventurer in Foch; the modern state is safe from its Generals. He was an absolutely dependable public servant. His glitter suffered from it;

no poor fools are going to go mad at the news of his death, as they did when that great persecutor of humanity, Napoleon, died. Foch neither amused, exalted nor excited the imagination; he was bread; not wine, to his nation and times.

I suppose that if he had cheated, exploited and enslaved his nation their emotion at the great pageant of his funeral would be even deeper. It is an old mastiff, a watchdog we have lost, not a hero; gratitude is not one of humanity's favorite emotions. But watching the gun carriage down the processional way every one, however normal, will feel as it passes his rank, at any rate, some certain shrinking of the heart, a loneliness at the thought that whatever fearful catastrophe we bring on or are thrown into by the merciless gods we must get out of by ourself, without the help of that brain, heart, and will, hitherto entirely at our service, trustworthy, unselfish and invincible, our old bodyguard, Ferdinand Foch.

✦ 31 ✦

The Gray Hands

CLEMENCEAU, as an episode of history, is one of the most extraordinarily interesting that modern history possesses.

But the noise of the grand finale of victory—success often banalizes the human significance of a life—has

132

The Gray Hands

quite drowned the singular, original theme of his story. Judge for yourselves. But first recall something more of the figure than the monocolor of his countlessly reproduced photographs.

As I recall him, I have a distinct impression that he was tall—that may be a deformation of memory, because the last and most impressive sight I had of him was hurrying beside Wilson and Lloyd George through a side exit to the Palace of Versailles, after the signature of the Treaty.

Tall, or only giving the impression of size, he had the most unexpected head in the whole gallery of Europe. For he did not look like a European at all. In his coloration, the bent of his expression, and strongest of all in an indefinable, unmistakable allure—probably not seriatim in his features, which may be why all the pictures miss it—he is a Mongol.

Not, please, a Chinaman, still less a Japanese, but some stronger, coarser, older branch, let us say the vanished tribe of Attila, of Genghis Khan. The French usually have a legend to account for this, about a lost squadron of Hunnish cavalry who took refuge and rooted in his native province, La Vendée, after their last battle, ages ago. Really a mighty face, and a dangerous face.

I think the only other detail that matters was his eerie habit of gray wool gloves, which no one for generations had ever seen him, morning or night, without. This thick gray padding of his hands, whatever it concealed, made all his gestures seem blindfolded, or groping, even the famous fists half closed on the table,

133

which affected the nerves of J. M. Keynes so much at the conference.

Now the world, and in a degree his own countrymen too, have forgotten that when the war broke out (and for at least a year thereafter) Clemenceau was a broken and disused old man. His explanatory career would be very interesting. But as hard and as long to relate to those uninitiated into the Balzacian complication of French political history as the Einstein theory, or some great game at the Bowl. He had started by being Mayor of Montmartre, the largest blood-pool of the Commune, during the troubles. He fled to escape the terrible vengeance of that other terrible old man, Thiers, and of course then came to America and there acquired one of his excessively few enthusiasms, outside ancient Chinese pottery, for the English-speaking world's ways.

Then you have the return and the incredibly long and consistent campaign of Cabinet wrecking, periods of power, and the smash over the Cornelius Herz revelations. So peculiarly irritating to the Paris prejudice, rather than particularly grave or extensive, were the charges against him in this great affair that his enemies and his three or four friends counted him a finished man forever. And, I quite suppose, he thought so himself until the war.

His dictatorship, though primarily a phenomenon of "last choice," was only attained after the most astonishing journalistic campaign; with only a fly-sheet, *L'Homme Libre*, to work with, he fought, wept, groveled, threatened, scrabbled with his hands into power, getting his chance to make war, just as a giant might fight to escape an agonizing death.

From here, every one knows the events, few the framework of terrifying possibility they clothe and conceal. I do not in the least refer to the trivial fact that he was a tyrant, that in side things, in satisfying private grudges and debts he stopped reluctantly. There is a case of much higher judgment. I will state it in a question.

What would have happened if Germany had had another Clemenceau, opposite? A dictator, that is, infinitely ruthless, utterly determined, neither to be moved by pity, without the least weakness of despair, who as long as he lived, whatever happened, whether all the chief cities and his capital were utterly destroyed, all the commerce ruined beyond hope of recovery, while a boy or man, with or without uniform, remained alive to hold a gun, would never have yielded? A man locked on one idea, who walled up every exit from the war except victory, at any cost, in any time? Who would have fought, as Clemenceau put it, "up to the frontier of the Pyrenees," if not with allies, without them; if all regular army organizations disappeared, with guerillas, franc-tireurs, bandits—whatever can kill? A man who had the will and the hands to keep his people to it?

Such was the gulf that the armistice covered over deep enough, certainly, not merely to cripple civilization, but to break its neck. For the historic moment of his power the world ran with its steering gear jammed —until Germany broke.

Now such a character, though rarely emergent on the grand stage of history, is rather obviously, it seems to me, in its main traits, a product of an originally strong and destructive will that has been characteristically deformed by age. Age may, and often does, weaken obstinacy, by the realization at seventy-odd years that most human things do not matter. So an old, old man, in power, will no doubt usually shrink from action. But he may, once in a while, like Clemenceau, moved inwardly by some under-hatred, some sub-rage, explained by the private incidents of his career, become for the same reason prepared to put mankind to death because he considers ruin, death, and all things of the same unimportance. The Senators of Rome, in the grand days, must have been men of this sort.

This Clemenceau is a historical fact; it is equally established that before he died he had already vanished, and that the appeased old man who was interviewed, cheered—more and more, as the old outline blurred with time, loved: that charming, venerable old fellow the press of the world was ready to eulogize in column-long obituaries, had taken his place. So the grimmest old citadel, with its turrets from which garrisons once poured down molten lead, its oubliettes, where prisoners long ago rotted to a slow death, at last becomes all overgrown with pleasant green creepers, and a show spot for tourists, old and young. His ferocious tongue had turned into an amiable gruffness, and his iron will only provided a cheerful moral lesson, full of philosophical gayety. Only the historian and the

nervous can now see a trace in the sight of anything
but the tranquil and the picturesque.

The Looting of Genghis Khan

O LD China is the treasure-seeker's next field, now
that Egypt is barred, and Yucatan and Nin-
eveh are under local-government boards. Dazzling
things have been brought in every cargo from Hong-
kong these seventy years, and every greater museum
and collection has had its share in them, but they are
comparatively modern, most not more than five hundred years old. Treasures of the older civilization, beyond any curator's dreams, wait to be dug for, almost
for the asking. On the hinder boundary of the Empire,
where the desert begins, there are whole cities under
the sands. The rustless air and the solitudes are keep-
ing them safe for archaeologists yet to be : boys as yet
perhaps, and only dreaming of the insignificant hoards
of Captain Kidd. Where are the caches of Genghis
Khan and those looters of the universe, the Golden
Horde? And those of the mighty pre-Christian Emperors and cities as old as stars, that preceded the
Mongol, through whose hands all the wealth of the
Greek-Chinese first trade routes passed? The porce-
lains, the bronzes, the jewels and the ivories and the
painted manuscripts, in strange tongues, we have re-

covered, are nothing to what remains laid up there, in the remote borders of China. Even the forty-six cases of scrolls in unknown script that Stein brought back, and the gallery of delights in the Cernuschi Museum, Paris, are only samples of what is in store. They excite us with their vague promise of other marvelous legacies, other Pompeiis, richer Ninevehs, stranger Valleys of Kings, like the sculptured tusk that Salvation Yeo brought back from the Spanish Main.

This Cernuschi Exhibition shows the finds of three men: Wannieck, the French archaeologist; those of Doctor Sire of the University of Stockholm, mainly statues and temple decorations; those of Major Lartigues, fragments of tomb sculpture. Wannieck has been at work since the war, through bad times in Chinese history. He has been far in the bandit country, and he has had wonderful luck. He had marked down the buried city of Chu-Lou-Sien, that was overwhelmed in an inundation of mud from the Yellow River, in A. D. 1110. The day that he arrived and was ready to go down into the trenches that peasant diggers had prepared, they brought him news that a landslip on Mount Ho-Chen near by had revealed a mass of ritual treasures, offered to the spirits of the mountain, one of those five sacred in old China, by the Emperor Tsin-Che-Hoang-Ti. Two priceless pieces of Wannieck's trove belonged to this mountain shrine. One, a round bronze pot with a cast frieze of figures, with three pointed feet, is coated by time with an exquisite patina of blue. It was in its making a satisfaction for the eyes. Damp centuries in the cliff-hollow have embellished it with a tint that is one of the unattainable colors of nature, like the back of a scarabeus or the breast of a humming-bird. No enamel in the world is the equal now of this rusted pot. In the same glass show-case is the chief piece in the collection. It is a sacrificial bull, the length of the hand, spotted with gold, with a splash of blue patina, not the ethereal azure of the pot, but the color at the base of a flame. The bull is lying with three legs bent, the fourth thrust out in front in ritual posture, waiting for the knife. So it must have appeared to the Emperor kneeling on his woven carpet, before the grotto in the sacred cliff. The maker of this little masterpiece, only in the line of the back and the poise, has put all the fat rich weight of the beast.

From the buried city Wannieck has brought hundreds of rarities: a cluster of porcelain beauties, fixed in gimcrack attitudes of dance; a bronze pig, with blue flowers on his fat, as if tattooed; bowls, jars, vases, as thin as shells, colored as tenderly as the inside of a plover's egg. There is a teapot, in the shape of a Buddhist lotus, with a cynical little puppy on top, milk colored. A head of some great lord or robber, bearded and purple lipped, his black hair in the form of an Asiatic mitre; the vision of the vigor of the senses. In these first diggings, the explorer found many tiled roofs, and faïence gargoyles of the rain gutters. One is a green horse, sitting up on its thick, strong legs, a laughing horse. Another is a fish goddess or mermaid, with sulky tired lips. In a courtyard he found an Imperial bowl, the tint of ripe grapes.

From a buried garden he brought a fountain, a carved lotus of aloof beauty in pink-gray granite, with a name and a verse inscribed in the Sutra script. A palette of rose clay, for ground-ink, in the shape of a tortoise without its upper shell, in whose complete simplicity are preserved all the secrets of design. In aquamarine glaze, there are figurines of ladies with lambs, sitting cross-legged. Their chignons are done up in lovers' knots, and round their necks are collars of large leaves. This was archaic China, nearer to us than much later days, and than the out-of-date work of our own artists twenty years ago. For good art is always modern: it is the empty ingenuity of bad periods that ages. All these treasures are perfumed with humanity. Any one of them would sweeten the whole life of a possessor, unless he were blind and deaf. They come from a world, different in its picturesque trappings, its wise old gardeners, its caravans of fierce Turcoman knights, fantastic Syrian monks of the Nestorian sect, and trade in strange stuffs; different from our modern material of life, but intimately familiar in its essence to our dreams. For the supreme fascination of such marvelous finds as Wannieck's, and Carter's, and Layard's in spite of the bashful veil of history and science that the archaeologists draw over them, is that at any moment may appear, from the layers of our rich mother earth, stuffed down to her tertiary strata with relics of other ages, the furniture and clear evidence of a Golden Age, to comfort us. They are rediscovering the Islands of the Blessed. Each of the greater finds reveals a civilization and a time more beautiful, more

140

desirable, than our own. This world of Old China, set against even the supreme elegance of Tutankhamen's Egypt, is especially delectable. Its ornaments in this exhibition fit into the haunting vision, that Arthur Waley in his translations of the ancient Chinese poets has already prepared, of life in gardens, where everything in the houses was as simple and beautiful as the trees. Our own age will not leave any such trace. In a thousand years, even if swaddled in preserving mud, our fragile leagues of railway will be rotted away, the brittle detail of our machines be quite corroded. Even in our own times, our possessions have a short life, and end unnoticed. Who knows what happens to our highest masterpieces, our automobiles, after their ten years' use? The other day, in a country fair in the center of France, I found the engine of the car that won the Paris-Milan race in 1910, clattering round to drive a noisy roundabout. With all our wonders, we will leave less of ourselves and our strange lives and whole civilization for the excavators of the future, than one Old Chinese Town.

✦ 33 ✦

Lilliput Lost

SERIGNAN is a faint dot on the map of Northern Provence, an accidental village grown on the immense shore of pebbles and bushes of the prehistoric

Mediterranean, now dried up. Within the distance of a baker's round of it stands the Harmas of Henri Fabre. Since the old man died—he was ninety-three— his books have sold better, especially in their English translation, and our rulers, yielding to the ever-alert Propaganda Office of Torrism, have classed his house as a memorial museum. His favorite daughter—she who used to toddle after grasshoppers for him with a paper trap—has been installed guardian, with a monthly pay, and the use of part of the house. It is she who now opens the door in the wall when you ring, shy and tiny, dressed in withered alpaca, and she who absent-mindedly unlocks the side wing, where her father wrote his life work. It is dusty, for she is old; and smells of mouldy old papers. A wretched refectory table, where glass cases with gaping joints betray some sticks of rotten wood, some shells of bumblebees and dung beetles lying in their nests on sifted sand, to the disintegration of the weather. Beside it, the bedroom table where he worked. It would creak under his hand now. On the deserted heights of the cupboards stacks of quarto papers on end, tied in packets between warped cardboards: his great herbarium which was never published. In the porch downstairs, the little girl who has grown so strangely old, points to a dark corner of the cobwebs; she says that father there hung the nests of his mason-bees. On one side still stands, where he forgot it, a crooked box riddled with reeds cut like a pen. This is the celebrated hive for the solitary bees where Fabre found the secret of the alternation of sexes in the egg. From this porch, we are allowed to diverge into the old man's drawing-room. The perishing paper on the walls, the backs of the family photograph frames, the leaves of the visitors' registration ledger—all impart in the closed room the vapors of mould and the past.

An invisible fog of this attar of melancholy issuing from the damp papers, the shut rooms, pervades for a distance the garden behind, where old-fashioned trees are running to seed and dead branches. Yews and cypresses and pines are growing into a jungle along with the impenetrable clumps of bamboos, that are rank and dark. In their shade, the stone dish of the fountain, where at the tag of their ordained journey over burning leagues of stone and sand, the male frogs hobbled under Fabre's eyes, their hind claws tangled in the gray bags of their eggs. The fountain, too, is green now, moss blurs its angles, and rags of green gelatine clog its water. Farther down, a scraped path trails out of the trees into the Harmas itself, that waste strip of bushes and gravel which was his true laboratory. Here the air has pulled itself free of all the mortal odors of the house. Everything is as he left it. The bleak sun shines on the wilderness of thyme and sage, the heated patches of sand between. There stands, still untouched by hand or weather, a tripod of sticks, a terra-cotta pot round whose rim he once led the hopelessly lost procession of pine-caterpillars for a week, in holy, scientific jest. In its bottom, he hung carrion to bring blowflies. Here on this flimsy altar of science he destroyed for us the most loathsome terror of the grave.

But this, like the books, the tables, the fountain, and the box, has but a few years to outlast him. Underfoot, ever renewed, so ever young, eternally the same, is the world he preferred, the universe of insects. Everything there goes on the same road, it has outgrown the laws of change, and mastered all decay. A stupid epigraph labels this man, "Homer of Insects." It is much truer that he was their Lemuel Gulliver. That snarling sea-dog could have spared his voyages and bent over a stranger Lilliput at the back garden of Serignan. Fabre, by simple bending of the neck, had underneath him an immense little continent, its forests, prairies, fields, inhabited by an uncountable population; an older, more crowded world than Egypt. The Harmas was his Africa; he knew it like his own garden. Here as it will be in a thousand thousand years is the enormous business of life; unconquerable tribes of insects are building, fortifying, excavating their inextricable passages under the earth, weaving and warring, with minute campaigns and infinitesimal commerces. He knew them all, as no living creature has known them. He was at home in their tiny landscapes, and practiced in their antediluvian customs: a remote god who for his own inscrutable studies it sometimes pleased to bring strange catastrophes upon his peoples, lifting them to fantastic voyages and supernatural adventures. Fleets of dragonflies brushed against his coat; armies of ants marched past his boot. On the inch-high hills beetles were grazing; in the grass forests, the black Lycose spier of Narbonne had its coverts. He knew their geography. He knew at least

the interjections of their vocabulary. The shriek of the
cicada stabbed to death by a grasshopper, the wing
notes of a spider-hunting wasp were as intelligible to
him as the faraway voices of the servants quarreling
in patois. For he was ninety years a resident among
their tribes. When the intermittent fever of his own
ambitions and resentments was upon him, when even
his sharp pen failed to relieve, he would crush on his
old black hat, and, black eyes ablaze, so that no human
dared to speak to him, he would return to the universe
in the Harmas. In contemplation of the unalterable
laws of their marriages and huntings, he found the
same lofty consolation as an astronomer among the
stars. Their geometric beauty, the engine-turned precision of their armor, could wean his mind from human
imperfections; in his life-long study of instinct, he
seemed to be watching the dance of living mathematics. In that study, that part of him which was immortal found its passion; it was his life from when,
but three years old, he lay on the grass for hours to
watch a scarab, till the windy day he died. First by
suspicion, then fully assured, he saw that the origin
of instinct is a very antechamber to the last mystery,
and at the door he knocked and entreated as long as he
lived, with a reverent despair.

Now he is dead, the stupidity he girded at so often
and petulantly has rewarded him. They have put up a
statue to him in the village he could not endure. They
have put his daughter on wage in his own house. These
things would have pleased the grim old man, always
starving for honors which never came. But they only

serve to bind tighter the things and the place that surrounded him to his own mortality. In part they reassure the swarming populations of his Harmas in the peace he so gently troubled. The ant castles and wasp-potteries are sheltered forever from the cataclysmic harrow of some peasant tenant. But for the rest, these honors keep the firmer the house, the trees, the fountain in that atmosphere of tangible decay, melancholy with his ghosts, into which the death of the house-master delivered them. Even for the insects, if they but knew it, far out of their sight, twenty whole yards back, hidden by the inconceivable altitude of the trees, their kindly god lies defeated by their mysteries, and dead.

✦ 34 ✦

The Recipe of France

IN spite of antique hygiene, a terribly patriotic press, passably corrupt politicians, and a certain cult of ill-bred young men, France is the most obviously pleasant place in the world for any stay from a week to a lifetime. Her delectable secrets have such quality that they out-charm her faults irresistibly from the mind even of those who hate them worst. Foreign puritans, pacifists, reformers are always sorry to leave Paris, though they find daily ten good reasons why they should go in disgust.

France does not end with Paris. The immeasurable charm exists through all her other great cities—Lyons, Marseilles, Bordeaux—growing not weaker, but simpler and more easy to understand as your distance increases from the capital, away from the vulgarity and noise of Montmartre and Montparnasse—which you begin to realize is mainly brought by the foreigner—away through her most modest market towns, to the heart of her innumerable villages.

The more unfashionable the traveler's road, the clearer and fresher become these secrets of France. And at last, in the hinterland of a lost province, he comes upon the roots and the fountain of the charm, that will work upon him as long as he lives. He will have lost sight regretfully of many delights that he imagined fundamental to France—her clear, gay literature, that in spite of Félibrige and regionalism evaporates to mere pastime away from Paris, her painting and her music.

One seldom hears singing in this country-side, and except in the cities there are no bookshops. But in shining simplicity three more fundamental arts, from which all the France which pleased him derives—architecture, dress, and cooking; those domestic arts, without which all the others seem unnaturally built in the air, appear every day of his wandering more exquisite, vigorous, original.

The French provinces, unlike those of any other country in the world (except, they say, China), are in full possession of all these elements of civilization, and so are in no possible bad sense provincial. Looking backward to Paris from a village of Limousin or Périgord, you do not see a model from which everything that is pleasant is imitated, but a derivative as if you looked to the wide mouth of a river from its source. The Rue de la Paix is the sum of the individual good taste of every peasant girl in France, shown in their historic and beautiful costume that still survives. The mighty *chefs* of Larue and Montagné are only improvers, in their most gorgeous banquets, of country dishes. And the Champs Elysées is an edition de luxe of one of these admirable market squares.

The frail grace of the untouched houses in French villages, the visionary beauty of the countless châteaux, the fountains and turrets and roofs, and the enduring taste of the common people, their mayors and country officers, which has preserved all this until our days in its unerring virtue, in daily use and freshness (unlike the unappreciated, exploited relics of Italy), is very thoroughly known: as is the rich legacy of folk-costume and festival shawls and lace, and all the elegances of Provence, Brittany, Creuse, Gascony.

But the country cooking it is not so much the fashion to praise. This is the region of truffles, and *foie gras,* and wine. In any one of a thousand villages you may enjoy such a meal, at any hour, as I have just finished. The villages have 700 inhabitants. There are three restaurants, equally good, and rivals: existing, mysteriously if you like, as the swarm of old masters did in Holland in the seventeenth century, not on the custom of rich foreigners, but on the natives themselves.

Tourists never come this way. There is nothing but

what is natural and proper to the countryside. Yet
the old hostess begins as a matter of course with an
omelette, with truffles, made with a spoonful of cream,
not to be bettered by any *cordon bleu*, fragrant, delightful. The truffles were found last winter by her own
old sow under the roots of the dwarf oaks at the bottom
of her meadow. They are the truffles of Périgord, black,
crisp, the same, with all the advantage of having escaped long travel, as are sold at gold weight in Pic-
cadilly.

There are goose livers, *foie gras au naturel*, con-
fected by herself and served with sliced lemon on a
white plate of old faïence. With these there is a golden-
brown roast chicken, stuffed with the magic herbs, the
traditional bouquet of Périgord, marjoram, wild mint,
sage, and who knows what.

In season there is always either a trout from the
River Isle that passes under the old bridge below, or
the "goose ham," *confit de foie*, pink, flaky, smothered
in its own savory grease.

Each village, though separated only by ten miles,
has its own luxury, its own delicacy. At Chatillon
there are lampreys, with sauce of mushrooms, herbs,
butter, like brown Venetian velvet. At another there
are ortolans or quails, or (to shock and bring water
to the mouths of partridge-shooting English women)
lark pies.

The whole of France could be mapped gastronom-
ically in local dishes, cooked with love and art, some
would say "only for peasants." It is a land of milk and
honey, the best milk and the most perfumed honey,

where all the good things of the earth overflow and are cooked to perfection.

The great dishes that figure in their native tongue on the tables of all the sybaritic millionaires and princes of the world are only copies of the daily menu of these happy peasants, who live in cottages that are miniature palaces for the art of their line and sculpture, and whose wives know how to dress.

The palate and the taste that runs through most French things, even the bad ones, provided they are not mere unintelligent imitations from the foreign, is surely founded on this art of good eating and the rest of good living, which survives as vigorously as their vines in the uncrowded, prosperous villages of France.

With all these joys and possibilities it is obvious, to those who know their humanity, that most of the young peasants long to fly to exile themselves in insalubrious suburbs, to exchange their local pies and wine, and spacious, noble, old kitchens, for the miseries and high wages of towns.

The French countryside is steadily emptying. At present it is the pleasanter for being uncrowded: the earthly paradise never had more than a couple of human inhabitants. And the old men who remain, and the prodigals who have returned with money and experience, are as yet sufficient to gather the rich crops and enjoy them.

One day, no doubt, if the process goes on, the tide of life will inconveniently slacken in these adorable villages, the old arts will decay from inanition. Then Paris itself, and the France as we knew it, will wither gradually, with the drying of the deep currents in the country which once fed it, with all its architecture, its taste, all its good things. And the life in great French cities which is now one of the world's most undisputed joys will become gradually like any other sort of life, in any other land.

Those days are distant. History, like one of these slow rivers, never runs straight as a canal, but abounds in bends and returns on itself, that embellish the banks with many a delightful reach, and secluded water, before the river reaches the predestined limits of its course, and the sea.

✦ 35 ✦

The Stone-Age Kindergarten

LES EYZIES, France.—This was a prehistoric lake: the Cave Man's Kindergarten. Cro-Magnon, Le Moustier, Les Madeleines, hamlets whose names have baptised whole epochs of prehistory, are spaced round its dried-up shores. The old lake is now the meadow valley of a slow river, grown high with bluish crops of wheat and clover this spring. The walls of limestone alone remain as they looked in the Stone Age, eaten into thousands of caves, holes, and grotesque shapes that peer out under the mask of dwarf oaks and black elders.

Here Nature pushes her face near humanity with

a friendly grin. Ice, rain, and weather have worked
the soft stone, like dough, into innumerable humorous
and kindly shapes. Each yard of the cliffs has its queer
appearance of natural sculpture. Above Cro-Magnon
there is a spur, grown over with yellow stone-crop,
that is in the unmistakable shape of Ally Sloper, the
English popular bogy. Round the bend at Les Madeleines, the Katzenjammer kids, malicious and rotund,
push plainly out of the bushes above the road. Like
a country shelf, round the whole valley there are set
imitations of all the comic, plastic jokes of common
humanity, sometimes like rough statuettes or whim-
sical heads, sometimes as if made for a rustic giant's
earthenware: Toby jugs, and beer flagons, and bowls
with crinkled sides streaked by the rain, as if the
indigo size had slopped over.

When the first ape-man found his way to this homely
place, after hard hunting in the unfriendly snow
wastes of the great plateau, these cliff sculptures must
have pleased and vaguely reassured him; he made it
his first home. The glacial lake in the midst promised
fish; the friendly gnarled cliffs invited him to climb
into its recesses and be safe with his mates and his
young. The relentless first gods suspended their hos-
tilities against him here at Les Eyzies. Everything his
glimmering humanity could desire was set conven-
iently near. At the foot of the caves were heaps of
orange-sized pebbles, brown outside and purplish
within, heavy flakable stones that broke to a point;
the best flint deposits in Europe.

They called to his Pithecanthropic hand to be used

for throwing and striking, his first weapons. Science has dug and sifted and washed the floor of these caves where ape-man lost his prefix; found the daggers and ax heads and mallets of his first manufacture, more precious than nuggets, and made this out-of-the-way place a prime pilgrimage for all who are curious about the beginnings of their kind. We are in humanity's cradle, where its first toys are scattered on the cave floors.

Cro-Magnon, where the skulls of three of the first men were found by a French surveyor, Lartet, in 1868, is now only an empty cavity under a rock at the side of the road. At Le Moustier, where Hauser, German excavator, found the Mousterian skeleton in 1908, has been left a cut of unsearched earth, where in thick slices, as carefully ruled as a ledger, you can see the successive litter of five epochs of humanity. At Laugerie Basse, on the north side, where the scientist J. Maury has built a cottage and garden for himself, in superior rivalry with the Swiss Family Robinson, in the very cave fearful ancestors occupied forty thousand years back, he has left intact an even more revealing cut for our education.

It is fifteen feet high; rises from the bottom of the mouldy, dark flint-weapon stuffed cave level of the Mousterian, through the sterile whitish layer that nature left for ten thousand years, when the roof fell in, through the higher strata of the Cro-Magnon, the reindeer man, the mammoth man, the man of the new stone and polished axes, even to the inconceivably recent deposits of the Gallo-Romans and the Middle

Ages. For these convenient caves of the old Eden have never been left uninhabited. To this day the Limousin peasants build their cottages against the cliff side that serves sometimes as massive roof, sometimes as impregnable back-wall. The village of Les Eyzies itself, with its dark, ruined château now a museum, is built half in, half out of these ancient cliffs. Past its gossipy brown roofs, that start out of the cliff in a crowd, like a parcel of superstitious old women full of tales and shadows, runs the road to Font de Gaume, the pictured grottoes of the first artists.

For our first ancestors were taken in nature's kindly trap of Les Eyzies; they used the flints in the security she had provided, grew in the scale of being century by century, till at last they learned from the stone sketches she had placed before their eyes, and climbed high into achievements of art. In this grotto, long and damp as an ice house, are superb witnesses of how much they had learnt even in the Cro-Magnon era.

They did not make these wall paintings for pleasure or decoration, but for serious business of magic and hunting. The nearer to exactness and life in the drawings the firmer, more certain hold the artist, and the men of his tribe who trusted him with the office, would have upon the animals he sketched and hunted. Hungry, half terrified at the twisted solitude of this deep, sacred hole in the cliffs, where no trace of habitation has ever been found, the artist man crawled on his empty belly, stone lamp in hand, and lumps of red ochre and black oxide of iron, with the ceremonial wild beast mask on his head, to put the spell of art upon

The Stone-Age Kindergarten

the great bison, the wild ox, the untamed horse, the mighty mammoth itself, and all the fauna of his heroic age. In these dark and airless crevices the paintings have stayed though even granite outside has changed its shape. They look at first like dull smears, red and black, but when you stare at them suddenly you see an eye, a nostril, the living magnificent line of a monstrous back. The bison stands before you, force and speed and jolt, represented, not reproduced, with a draughtsmanship equal to Rembrandt and Hokusai.

Cro-Magnon hunted with flint arrow and reed bow; a savage more aboriginal than the Boesjesman or the Australian black-fellow, but he had the eye, the hand, the soul. To those who have seen only inevitably falsified reproductions of these paintings in books, the attainment of these first artists beyond even our own in its degree, is a theoryless mystery. Here, on the spot, you notice things which few scientists have mentioned. It was nature, that mysterious god which had provided their cave paradise and their flint beginnings, that guided their hand on the new art. She had set in her natural sculpture of the rocks, in rough shapes of animals and heads, the first idea of art in man's mind. And she set in the natural veins and marks in the rock side the commencement of his grotto paintings. Each of the designs I have seen, whether bison, or wild cat, or mammoth, has as its foundation line, some natural streak or ridge in the cave wall.

So through the ages of Neolithic man, who lost the trick of this strange mastery of art, but polished his axes, and built his dolmens and river cities, until the

Children of the Sun came, from Egypt, with the priceless mystery of metals, and began our day, through all the modern histories of Empires and adventures, these first paintings remain, the first records of man's long climb from the Ape, in the lime-stone valley of Les Eyzies, the cave-man's Eden.

+ 36 +

Easy Ascent

THE hillock that lifts up the spherical gleaming mounds of the Jesuit Church of Notre Dame loftily over immense Paris, is one of the pivots of mankind, whether you, or the moralists, or even its French owners like it or not. It is not venerated nor even respected. It is called Montmartre, that is enough. Millions of men, scattered in adventures over the whole globe, who would not set a foot forward on any other pilgrimage, dream one day of reaching Montmartre for that one night which is to repay the fever of Africa, the ice of Labrador, the price of all the fatigues they have expended to afford it. It is the dream-goal of that unrepentant animal in humanity that makes pioneers, gold-seekers, fortune-builders of all breeds work for the simple motive of future illimitable pleasures, and so, believe Kipling, do their share in the world. The hard men, the tough fellows who have no illusions, your

156

healthy undoubting materialists, look steadfastly toward Montmartre for comfort.

Every night, all the year round, new crowds of sensualists mount the steep cobbles to their Hill. Whichever of twenty streets they take, there is the same jolting view of seven-storied houses set on the ramp, seven tiers of wrought iron arabesques round the sills, over flashing rows of provision shops. Then a squadron of tiny hat shops. Then the outliers of the cabarets. Tall stage Cossacks on sentry go outside their shows. Green pages on the street-edge waiting for taxi-cabs, with the pill-box caps British Lancers wore at Elandslaagte in 1898. Then fatally we arrive either at the Place Pigalle, or the Place Blanche. Pigalle has a chilly fountain; Blanche, the yawning well-shaft of the Underground Railway. In summer, by the fountain, the dazzling, deceptive Church of Sacré Cœur shows above all the lights, like a false tiara; in winter, three of its pinnacles surmount the mists, in the reflection of the sky signs, like ruby scarf-pins.

Montmartre, this world pivot, is one long street on the side of the Hill, with unequal crooked satellites hanging down towards the City, like a worn-out comb. Within the space of its oblong mile are the total pleasures possible for the uneducated man. This concentration has grown out of the old suburb where the jolly families of 1830 used to picnic. In those days it was crowded with mills, and the rich millers who monopolized the trade of Paris lived well and gaily. It was

a frontier. When the steam mills grew up, it was cut
into building lots. A new slum was added to Paris;
part of the needy intellectuals migrated there with
their studios, eating-houses, *café chantants*, and mys-
tifications. And the gigantic red-haired Salis opened
his Black Cat. This *Chat Noir* is the first of the cabarets. It made Montmartre. Gradually the rich diners-
out, who hang on the artist crowd like children round
an organ-grinder, in the eternal hope of being amused,
found their way to the Hill. Moralists denounced it,
and its fortune was made. The first settlers, like Red
Indians, were pushed into reservations on the other
side of the Hill, where they still keep some doubtful
hold on the inaccessible slope. But all the rest, the
cabarets and dancing-places, whose names keep a taste
of the grossly cheerful days of Old Montmartre (forty
years old) are given over to the rich, foreign pilgrims.

The Dead Rat and the Rat which is not Dead, the
Red Mill and the Cake Mill, and all their progeny of
Blue, Green, and Russian Mills, these keep no other
trace of their variable origins but their names. It is
one of the properties of Montmartre that time passes
quickly there. A cabaret that is three years old is an
historic curiosity. Such places as the Cabarets of
Heaven and of Hell, and of the Grave, that date from
the last Exhibition when blasphemy was amusing, and
a *papier maché* skull gave a shiver, have an indefinable
air of antiquity, not the precious aroma of centuries,
but the shabby, premature aging of a clown. They
have fallen in two short decades from the vice of the
rich to peepshows for provincials. Montmartre has a

mosaic of such seedy, cast-off cabarets, that hang on to the cloaks of the glaring, brand-new night haunts, as the draggled sluts of the pre-war now cling desperately near the doors where Something is going on.

Unmindful of these vestiges, the man who has come from Arizona or Central Africa, undeviatingly mounts the right stairs, to the latest, the dearest, the supreme feasting-places of last season. Fat carpets, saxophone bands, smooth floors, plush seats against the wall, are their unchanging regalia. In each the principal ornament is a nickelled champagne bucket, filled with ice. Each has its gallery of business-like beauties, nonchalantly waiting for someone to pay their dinner. The range of material pleasures is limited. Man's brains have transformed the earth and the sea, but sensuality remains where it was before the flood. Women; wine; noise. The whole wonderful scope of French cooking is too learned, too artistic for Montmartre, where nothing is eaten but Chicken and Oysters, nothing drunk but Champagne. For the rest, there are the girls; the management sells children's toys, colored celluloid balls to throw, and blue and red paper streamers, with paper caps, dolls, and the usual amusements of an infant birthday party. The man who has come a thousand miles for this is contented. For the glorious champagne that seems to freeze in the glass as the foam subsides is a famous trickster. Not only for the quick, certain profit do the managers of Montmartre insist on this wine alone being served. Without it, the sum of this world's pleasures might appear a little thin. But the butler bustles, the girls wake up under cross fire of celluloid marbles, and follow up the paper streamers to their end in the hand of flushed, tanned foreigners preparing for another throw.

The great illusion lasts till dawn. Half an hour less, I am told, would ruin more than the fifty per cent. of cabaret managers every year. Economically, in spite of the vast free publicity made for Montmartre, in spite of the ferocious pluming of the visitors, fortunes are rare in the business. The swarms of parasites which each cabaret must support, the incompetence, dishonesty, folly of the staff from waiters to kitchen boys, eat most prospects of profits. But it goes on, must continue. For without what Montmartre stands for, countless honest, hard-working men would not know what to dream to do with their money.

At dawn Montmartre is different. It is tired out. All its shams are taken off. The streets are empty of the raving, noisy detail of the night before, and one can notice at ease the *répertoire* of the hour. A drunken Englishman is being huddled into a taxi. The fountain has frozen. Sly shadows are pulled across the empty street; sewer rats on their business, hungry Montmartre cats after them. A woman of sixty, raddled to the eyes, is leaning against a lamp-post absently, quite forgetting where she is. A policeman swings his arms and yawns. In the Rue Victor Massé, a high-voiced, earnest wrangle between women. The chiffonniers are busy in the rubbish boxes, hurrying to pick out what they want before, with a rumble and a clatter round the corner, come the Municipal scavengers to clear up before day.

The Deslys Mystery

THERE are people and careers who compete with the finest novels: nature's novels, and if you can get out of your head the prejudicial statement of the case by Oscar Wilde, you have to say that some of them bear any comparison.

These natural masterpieces, furthermore, seem to me more likely to resemble novels than really good short stories. For the latter is really the most artificial form of writing that there is, more so even than a sonnet. It is mysterious that there is a constant resemblance between the natural product and the prevailing school of novel-making in the country in which they occur. A real life in England might be obviously in the Dickens style, full of wills and humorous interventions of fate. But it is more likely to be faded and blurred halftone, like the work of all who have preferred since to follow Trollope.

The best of them, I think, come from France. But, then, I prefer Balzac and Flaubert, and even the nonhomiletical chunks of Zola. There is a common style irresistibly noticeable between the real lives of great French rogues and adventurers, and manufacturers and actresses, and politicians and criminals, and French novels. Which imitated which is no speculation of mine.

The latest really remarkable effort of nature and

history there is certainly the life of Gaby Deslys, which has now arrived at the antepenultimate chapter, where the plot thickens for the last time, in the French courts.

I wonder who remembers poor Gaby at all clearly now, outside her country—whatever that really was, to be sure, for there is the denouement. I do myself well. . . . I saw her dance five or six times. I saw her film her last piece, standing only about a foot behind the camera, at the old Casino de Paris. And I once spoke to her for some minutes.

She was of course very pre-war. Dancing particularly showed, as we can see now, a hectic flowering to greet the vast disaster that heated the air of 1913, as approaching earthquakes do. There were Nijinsky and Pavlova; even the music-hall was full of fever and energy. Gaby was one of its largest unseasonable blooms.

Not that she could dance very well. She was one of that rare but well-known species of genius which it always puzzles the world to estimate: creatures of vast animal energy. In the best kind this does not disperse itself at all in mere nervousness. There is nothing fidgetty about them. The force within is radiant. You can feel it at a distance, like an electrical warmth. Its characteristic effect is indeed to impart itself on its surroundings, like a constant bubbling of ozone. Even when they are silent, these human dynamos, there are sparks in the air about them. They wake you up, make you feel; irritate often, but never fail to galvanize. In short, they are undirected geniuses, for they seldom do anything you can put a pencil point on and call great.

A very beautiful woman hardly ever leaves a clear-cut impression of feature and shape in the memory. Usually there remains only an aura, a living color. Gaby was blondeness, and a pinnacle of great ostrich plumes—her symbolic headdress.

But all beauty and force need a prestige, too, and this she had. A very curious one, which you would never think could be acknowledged and esteemed by the British public, as nevertheless it was. She was a survival, as her native place, Marseilles, is a survival of a large, archaic moral manner. That is, she was one of those courtesans whose lineage runs parallel with the romance of history, right from the early middle ages, through the Pompadours to the carriage ladies of the Second Empire, the companions of Cora Pearl.

Whether King Manuel of Portugal really lost his throne through and for her is a matter of sentiment, not strict history. But that was the fable which entranced Europe, even, as I said, England. There was a slight tinting of awe in the way they felt, as there is in the superb pleasures of a Christmas tree all lit up for the babies. When she stepped on the stage it was all a dazzle—hair, jewels, feathers, silk, smile, like a fascinating but pagan goddess. If you remember, Barrie in one of his most ecstatically sentimental moments, somewhere in the war, wrote a play specially for Gaby. She had to push a perambulator and wear an apron. I don't defend that, but you can see the quite simple idea. She had a zurzurring Marseilles French accent which was the icing sugar on this cake. But, you see, anyway, she was not in the most trifling degree vulgar. Her loudness was musical.

She died soon after the war, and they sold her flat in London. No one was surprised (and yet only Princes and grandees had seen it) that her bed was solid silver, chased into the form of a shell or something, with a ten-foot crucifix in bog-oak at its head; and her bath was either gold, or onyx, or something, I forget what.

She left her large fortune—all the truly great courtesans, unlike mere gutter-cats like Nana, were never wasteful—to her mother and to the poor of Marseilles.

And then, what do you think? A family turned up in Hungary to claim that she was really their daughter, Edwige or Hedy Navratil, no relation to the Marseilles mother. The whole of Paris and France laughed at that. Do you think they would not have known? Harry Pilcer especially, and the lawyers who swore she was Gabrielle Caire by birth registration. It seemed one of those crazy cases and dropped, until this week. But now the claimants have found that in the Tout Paris social directory of 1915 she was set down, as "Deslys . . . real name Hedy Navratil." She herself supplied the information. Further, that the date of her birthday and year coincide with this Hedy Navratil's.

But that does not end it. The defendants have evidence that at the time of her glory there is legal proof of the existence of another Hedy Navratil, a dancer too, living obscurely in Spain and condemned to death in absentia by the Austrian Government as an Allied spy.

✦ 38 ✦

Romance

THE death of Frau Zubkoff, once Princess Victoria of Schaumburg-Lippe of the House of Hohenzollern and sister of the German Kaiser, ends her tragic variant of the old story. As for Zubkoff, he is in Bonn jail to answer charges of vagrancy, false pretenses and petty theft.

I should think it possible that the strange things that have happened in the world in the last fifteen years have affected the secreted individualities of royal houses more than any other people of the world. This Princess seems to have been all the time a charming and romantic creature, all through the years she was known to the world only as one more of those unrevealing social actresses who make up the inner circle of all royal houses.

All the time that she was playing cautiously under the eyes of gorgon governesses in the inner gardens of castles or riding in Kings' parks, or later on setting models of deportment for the dancers who were enjoying themselves at state balls, traveling in state,

165

and never allowed to bore herself alone or unaided in the unlivable apartments of the Kaiser's chain of palaces, she must have been premeditating love and liberty and the life out of her favorite story books.

We are sluggishly disposed to believe that such personages felt the war and history's postscript to it less than ourselves, if at all. Do you think the Prince of Wales would have dared to elude marriage before the war? Or that the King of England does not feel night and day the death of his cousin, the Czar, and all that family? That King Alfonso of Spain feels, one way or another, less the fate of the King of Italy under the Mussolini régime than you do the most spectacular losses of your friend in the stock crash? There is no public so news-hungry, so fascinated with the last detail of events of the life outside as the inmates of a prison. These royal people are prisoners in a way, and there was a fire in the jail.

And so the Kaiser's sister herself, in the wing that burned down, found herself free to go into the big world, which books and the naïve reasoning of her heart told her was an infinitely real and wide place. It is quite common for such an education to produce, even, a sort of palace Red, a believer in the most guileless chapters of liberalism and even Socialism. You can see traces of this even in that old sea captain, King George. Or you need not let your eye wander and content yourself with the continual row of millionaire young men and debutantes, who pass across the news by fits and starts on the tracks of Don Quixote, to save that distressed maiden, humanity.

Romance

This Princess saw the flight of the Kaiser, the ruin of the army, the vanishing of all the great lords and families from power, and it was as if walls were down in an earthquake for her. She took timidly at first to voyages of exploration in liberty, to concerts unaccompanied, and then when she saw it was true it did not matter, to theatres, picture galleries, shows and night clubs.

It is a characteristic of a royal education (and even of a billionaire one) to be a generation late in the arts. In the great ages the great are the leaders of taste; in our own which has lasted ever since the eighteenth century, their favor is a superannuation of and not a premium on genius. So, like her British cousins, Victoria of Schaumburg-Lippe was brought up with the concept of the decrepitude of art. She went straight from Christmas cards of wassail and three-deck ships and academy portraits to the rattle and bang of the modern school. This too excited her beyond endurance.

Therefore, the result of the emergence of this myopic soul was not disappointment, but an extremely strong conviction that the life outside was much better than she had ever imagined; that the whole of her hopes and theorized dreams, guaranteed by what her eyes could see, must be inexhaustibly true.

That is to say, when she met Zubkoff, it was she, the middle-aged lady, who was young, spiritually, almost to girlishness. He was exactly in the same way very old. The mysterious beauty of these temporary youngsters, dance partners, gigolos, gold diggers of both sexes may be caused, just as if they were legendary vampires, by the fact that in an exterior, young in skin and time, there is an aged soul, the soul of a wretched old skinflint swindler, some crook-fingered miser who had reduced the whole constitution of the universe, not to forces or molecules, but coins.

Let those who can feel it enjoy their beauty—for myself there is always some small thing wrong in their appearance that gives the devil away, a murderer's thumb in the golden night hostess, a vulgar jaw line in the varnished boy, like the old hoof that peeped out of the stocking heel. But when you are as young as the Princess Victoria, a Zubkoff is a fairy Prince. The smell of kitchen grease and the sink to her likes is quite concealed by Quelques Fleurs, or brilliantine.

Now, the great majority of these Cophetua romances that smash, I am convinced, are from the same difference of spiritual age. The wizened old souls in young bodies ruin the innocent new borns in wrinkles, gray hair, inclination to sag. Zubkoff was one of the worst of these vampirine youngsters, just as the Princess was one of the most kindly, irritatingly sweet of the victims. Zubkoffs, like this monster, are not only swindlers in that they steal, forge, extort money, in an insatiable sucking process from the first day of conquest. They, like he, never give the slightest return in tenderness, romance, just fun of life. Would you find a filthy old miser, an aged blackmailer and receiver of stolen goods good company for a dance?

So our Zubkoff never gave the great and unfortunate lady who had fallen into his power a moment which it would be tolerable to go over in the memory. It is true I once saw a photograph, when the gush sisters and brethren of the press were trying to make some banal conformation to the formula out of the match, with both of them standing beside his motorcycle; the first thing she bought him. Dear boys, dear hard-boiled girls, they all make for the quick transport, even before the new clothes, the pearls and the furs; because it is the dream of their class, as love is of their victims.

Well, now the story is over, with her in her grave, the Kaiser nursing his mangled self-love, and Zubkoff, unshaven, gross already—it is a comfort his likes do not last long or the world would be destroyed —snoring in the Bonn lockup.

✦ 39 ✦

The Circus Again

SCENTS wake up the personal memory just as sounds, the material of music, stir those venerable abysses of the mind that Jung discovered. The circus makes a clear, direct use of both major evocations to create its mood. If ever it evolved in the natural line of its trajectory so as to dispense with the sight of wild beasts, I suppose the best ones would still keep an elephant and a couple of lions simply for their odor, somewhere where it could reach the nostrils of the audience—the ammoniated musk that is the signal for the great nostalgia as soon as you enter.

For I believe that that nostalgia, that undefinable homesickness, as vague as the beauty of the sound of a horn heard in the deep of a forest, is the supreme quality of the pleasure of the circus. In such deep matters—and there are no deeper, more mysterious, nor important things in the world than the spiritual nourishment of the mind through pleasure—the surest, if not the very best (which are conscious works of genius), are produced without calculation or conscious effort, as a dancer crosses the high wire. The scenarists of the circus certainly do not intellectualize the steps to their effect; if they did they probably would fall into the net.

But everything in this circus atmosphere, which throbs and wells around you the moment you enter, is an almost unendurable tickling of the sense of the past. The first claim the advertisements snatch at is that their show is "old-fashioned." No one would want to see a brazenly modern circus any more than a modern cuisine, or a confessedly newfangled religion or a brand new constitution of laws. There is something pitiful in the heart of man which directs all its longings backward; paradise is to be regained, not created. The law must base itself on the ancient rights of man.

Dr. Adler the psychologist, with his usual canniness, observes that the kernel of this longing is "the desire of spoilt children to return to a more favorable situation in the centre of families." Doctor, every one was once spoiled, for we all once had youth, and nature petted us with the choice first fruits of feeling. No matter how poor, monotonous and hungry, every millionaire is homesick for his boyhood. And nations and states, in the midst of riches and progress, dream back to their rustic age. The further they have gone the more this irresistible sentimentality works in them. And so New York, of all places, loves the circus, that utterly agricultural, horse-wagon festival, the most of any place in the world.

The very band has a calliope and plays tunes from Sousa's repertoire, and Sousa took care to include "Maritana" and airs from the "Bohemian Girl" and "Der Freischuetz," "Silver Threads Among the Gold," "Scenes That are Brightest," "Then You'll Remember Me." With extreme simplicity everything there contrives to pick you up and dandle you back to the age of innocence.

The circus voice, with its echoing melancholy, talks to you like the one the dying Chinese Emperor heard on his golden bed, "Do you remember this, do you remember that?" until the sweat stood out on his forehead. The smell, the tune, the same old barefooted banquet of peanuts, crackerjack, popcorn. The ropes from the ceiling, shaking and dangling, the great rope nets which flap into place like sails. The clowns, the horses, the very sawdust patterned with their tracks, everything is the same. Almost indiscreetly the same, as if it were trying to make you cry.

And there, with the same flourish, so theatrical and conventional that it never had an atom of pose, the

Belle Equestrienne still rides in. The spangled, trunk-hosed comeliness, the divine first anima, to whose curves our tender senses first warmed, to whose by no means to be ashamed of ideal our raw hearts first warmed. These women of the circus—what blood that would be to boast of in a family tree! I would rather have had in my ancestry one of these magnificent creatures, who proved the purity of their blood, the sincerity of their hearts, the almost fabulous regularity of their lives, every night under a death penalty, than the most fanciful romantic combination of mere gypsies, Princes, sailors and poetesses all combined. I must be careful of my words now or I shall be claiming that they are my unique ideal of women. But just observe the immateriality of their ambition, the extraordinary rarity of the way of life that is acrobacy. I do not know which to admire most for the strangeness and almost poetical dignity of the occupation they make their life—as removed from the vulgar as a Queen or an anchoritess—the tight rope or the trapeze.

The French books say that the art of the rope was invented and brought in by, of all people, the Turks when they came to Europe, that dark and once invincible race of horsemen who may have thought of it when the extreme triumphs in acrobatic horsemanship no longer satisfied them, and they had to have something still more dangerous, super-human, to exercise their pride. You can still see their relationship and their artistic, but not natural and romantic, superiority to the earlier heroics when the girl in the air, with a

172

pole she does not need, struts and minces with exactitude greater than a ballet dancer, high over death, while around the ring, immeasurably far down beneath her, race her sisters, straddled on the saddles of two horses, shouting and whooping.

But then there also is the art of the trapeze, in which for brief hair-raising moments women and men become birds. This is one of the blindest and most impossible ambitions of humans—to have wings, to be freed from the touch of earth and water, the elemental harness of weight and clog. In airplanes we do not realize it—they are not birds but insects, giant dragonflies, if you like. Only in the triple somersault is a human being the equal of a bird.

There are many things altered in the circus of today. I was glad to see it. The show is not an archaeological curiosity; it is a living thing, and only part of the audience has memories to be worked on. While we who can remember taste our own privileges of emotion, thousands more are coming to it new. Perhaps they, the boys, not we, are the real heirs of the circus, they who are now storing food for memory, piling up treasures of things to remember and regret. We will not quarrel. The naphtha lamps are gone now, but I can smell them, all right. Smells, as I said, aid the imagination of memory. The talking clown is gone too; well, the strange rout, the masque of giants, dwarfs, nightmares of the comic, which has succeeded him is just as good. Even when they cut the gladiators out of the program in Rome it did not spoil the circus.

✦ 40 ✦

Van Gogh

ART abhors competition, which no bad critic can remember. So no one should really say that Vincent van Gogh is better than Gauguin, Seurat and Cézanne.

Nevertheless, there is a sort of primacy of his brilliance; by what is certainly rather an optical illusion, his proximity makes Gauguin seem a trifle literary, Seurat tired and even Cézanne rather plain.

This is one of the unfairnesses of the unique toward the only rare. For this young Dutchman, unlike his peers who were masters, had no school and no disciples, any more than William Blake in poetry. Van Gogh was Robinson Crusoe in a universe to himself, with all the consequences of isolation. He is outside the great continuity of art. Like Blake, he might have imitators, but never pupils. Unlike Cézanne, he is no structural part of the grand tradition of painting—only a blazing ornament tied on its wrist.

There is no secret that this lonely eminence of originality in his case has some root in his insanity. Madness alone is entirely free from the commonplace. However terrible or twisted or invalid the visions of sick brains, each is individual and new.

His affliction was, indeed, whatever its causes, on which the doctors are still differing, for the great part of his life a light one—no more, except in two or three

174

evil leaps upon him, the last of which ended him, than an approaching and receding cloud of melancholy. He could not, as he says in his remarkable correspondence, for long times at a stretch adapt himself to daily contact with strangers. But in Provence, where the best of his creative years as well as most of his blackest miseries were set, he went among the people and passed as one of them. Only a little more boastful at times, a little more apt to unreasonable silences in between, than that slightly touched race, the Provençaux.

I have seen the asylum at St. Remy-en-Provence where he found refuge, and where many of his master works were painted. I have even been allowed to visit his own little room. There is always to me a fantastic, grown-up innocence of atmosphere in such a place, quite different from yet of the same spiritual class as monasteries, barracks, settlement houses—all places where the inhabitants are separated in their lives from the cheerful commonplace of the world.

He has painted the iris bed in the cloister of this asylum (it was once a monastery and an architecturally charming one). One look at this inspired representation of that hidden, gorgeous, semi-secret flower garden would put before you the other-worldly strangeness of the place; of all such places, which from their proximity to many dreams have kept an indefinable unearthliness.

This also is in many other of his paintings, perhaps especially in that unforgettable "Room at Arles," with the brown bed covered with the coverlet, the color of arterial blood, which is a whole house, a whole city, for the soul to live in if it is not afraid to be alone; in his portrait of the gigantic bearded postman, whose uniform is of a blue that no one ever saw in the world, so fresh and deep and new, until Van Gogh mixed it.

But there is another and still more unplumbable quality in his pictures. If I tried to explain what every one can see for himself, and feel a little frightened at, very likely, I would have to choose it to be somewhere in the light, half-reflected, half-emanating, from his cypresses in his "Chasm," his "Les Paveurs." It is somehow as if he saw and reproduced not the natural light of common day, but the torrents of reflection of a more vigorous fire from a new planet, bigger, brighter, than the sun, and much hotter. Somewhere outside his canvases there is the illumination of a catastrophe in the cosmos.

And a wind from another planet, not of this earth, is what twists and shakes his great cypresses. This tree is the most difficult one to paint—no student will learn any trick of doing it from Van Gogh's monstrous success. His cypress is a green and yellow fire, with a purple glow at its heart, like a conflagration on a stem. It is full of the movement which is life deep inside its mass, but also, like all things that blaze, its surface forms instantaneous mosaics of dark and light.

It is this proximity of mighty things unseen outside, not inside, which is the highest merit of Van Gogh, and the measure of his vision to attain to. But how are they to be made a lesson or a model?

The Artist

Now they are here, arrived to us, framed, and iconolatrized by reverential multitudes, with the approval of all the sincere taste of the world, it is hard to imagine how they could ever be ignored, as they were, or patronized, or usually laughed at. Any hypothesis would lead us straight to the sore spot of all aesthetics: the virtually inevitable failure of criticism to recognize or even tolerate a genius on his arrival. These paintings to-day seem to have no doubt in them; they could have been hated, we think, but how, possibly, passed over?

But for this stupidity of the world Van Gogh was paid, as Blake was paid, by the inestimable advantage of being, until the day he died, artistically free. Art in a garret, or in a ditch, can at any rate grow freely. No wish to please, no entangling advice or encouragement, which has more often been destructive to original genius than mockery, ever came to corrupt his novelty or conventionally deform it. He was robbed of his reward, that is all: the least part of a career that is, after all, not entirely earthly.

The Artist

NOEL COWARD, if he goes on growing, is likely to be one of the most generally interesting representatives of our time, since his renown is steadily freeing itself from all allure of eccentricity and mere fashion.

I especially admit the new gesture of his talent, of which "Bitter Sweet" is a perfectly executed phase. It seems to me to be an instructive instance of the really true artistic attitude, which I should like to restore to the equipment of criticism.

To me, and no intellectual monopolist has said it since Bishop Percy and Charles Lamb, a true artist can be picked out of the bewildering mass of clever forgeries with which the market is flooded, especially to-day, by a rule of thumb—that he is unself-consciousness. I know that the bald statement is known and unluckily has been the excuse in a misinterpretation of its meaning for the degraded worship of naïveté, childishness, underestimation, writing down, and knowing appearance of non-trying, which is the plague of all the arts to-day, and which will make, I swear to it, the vast majority of our production as unbearably boring as that other critic-ridden, mock-modest body, the poetry of the English middle-eighteenth century.

Such, whether it manifests itself in deliberately unmelodious music, carefully bad drawing, short-sentenced fiction that insistently never raises its voice and never sheds a tear, is to me obviously the worst sort of self-consciousness, the vanity that apes humility, the sentimentality that substitutes a blow to the jaw for a literary gush that the authors really feel.

The spiritual posture of Coward that I mean in my definition is entirely bent over the audience, without

a thought of himself. That is, his motive is solely to
amuse, interest, stir, and never does he trade with the
thought, even, whether those he is so affecting with
the work of his heart and brain must think he is clever,
original or extraordinary, or not.

So worked the great artists of all time. Such was
the maker of Tutankhamen's throne and the anonymous ballads. And such is the reason why we do not
know Homer's real name or birthplace, nor the life
of Shakespeare. The desire for personal admiration
may possibly occasionally exist in a true artist, but
as a psychological disease, an infirmity—the last,
Milton said, to attack noble minds.

So, then, the immature sophisticates who whisper
to you with a bright smile that the tunes and the plot
of "Bitter Sweet" are not "strikingly" original invite
your sneers: Coward did not intend to impress you,
but only to give you that superb generosity, so much
more than the price of a ticket, that good artists are
incomparably more to be grateful to than any hundred million surplus scattering millionaire—a good
show.

Specifically, a romantic show. Instead of harrowing
you, as the legendary Russian Countess was harrowed
who let her coachman freeze to death waiting for her
outside while she wept over the dramatic sufferings of
injured goodness, in her box, Coward has chosen the
much more difficult, subtle and all-conquering motive, quite near Aristotle's idea of the role of tragedy
itself, of arousing that delicious and noble melancholy of the feeling of the past. This "restoration of

the years the locust hath eaten" is one of the hardest as well as sublimest of artistic enterprises.

It is, in fact, the predominant enterprise of poetry itself, resting, I surmise, on the profound, obscure human fact that the real savings and possessions of all our lives are simply an accumulation of beautiful, endearing scenes, tunes, for the memory. He chose as his main instrument (for the near past has more of the evanescent perfume than the more remote) the waltz. Was there ever a better instrument?

The very rhythm itself of this enchanting, mysterious measure, its haunting, three-footed dactyl seems to contain, as surely as tea roses smell sweet, the very attar of the consolation of lovely regret. Do you remember, those of us who danced before the war, to have seen ever one of the most exquisite of our debutantes, yes, with her program and pencil-favor tucked into her little bosom, moved to the strange ecstasy that comes just before crying by the deep, strange things the latest music was saying of change and memory? Yet it might have been her very first dance, poor one.

There is in this form—and Coward has put the last drop of it, your heart will tell you incontrovertibly, as well or better in the highest gallery seats at a matinee—into the whole music of this play, pressed down and brimming over, this vaporous, longing beauty. You see long-chilled couples in his audiences (and nobody's fools) looking at each other differently—sharing together in the reward of living for once. That is a widespread quality.

Green Pastures

You find it faintly when you look over old letters
the rats have nibbled at, one evening you don't go
out; there is a little of it, impure and odorous, in the
very sound of barrel-organs, in quiet squares in the
evenings, puffing out in gusts that intoxicate your
heart. It is all right for beasts to have no memories;
but we poor humans have to be compensated.

✦ 42 ✦

Green Pastures

FOLLOWING the immemorial etiquette of the
art of enjoyment that the good wine should be
served last, this aging New York season (1929–30)
presents us only now with the best play of the year:
Mr. Marc Connelly's "The Green Pastures." In one
night he himself, the season and our entertainment
have attained the first class.

It is singularly difficult to analyze what has intensely moved the mind either to enthusiasm or hatred.
Yet that is a sort of duty, the only one perhaps laid
on its beneficiaries by true art. Mr. Marc Connelly's
play will bear a great deal of meditation before the
simple sensation of fascination is broken up into its
constituents. I think the most wonderful part of it is
perhaps that he, a white man, a New Yorker, a highly
civilized man, should have been able to write and produce it. For the presentation of a Negro cosmogony is

fuller of dangers and crevasses than the approach to the South Pole. Not one of themselves has yet been able to achieve this, the inner mysterium of their culture; it is at the same time deep and innocent, full of humor, without the slightest touch of the ridiculous, primarily human, yet specifically racial.

What he had to do was that formidable enterprise: to write a miracle play. Twenty years ago such talents as Claudel and Yeats failed at the task. Yet as a super-difficulty Mr. Connelly tried for not a European miracle play—the mere tour de force of going back to our own middle ages, in which he would be helped by his own subconscious memory, huge masses of information and innumerable models—but to reveal in this hard form the secrets of that strange, poor people who make you cry when they sing and laugh when they talk, the American colored people. This measures the extent of his success.

His path first led straight through that incredibly narrow channel which lies between the sublime and the comical, the truly vulnerable spot in the heart. His heaven, that is, had to make you laugh in a peculiar way—the way you laugh at a baby, or the walk of an elephant, or any other innocent yet venerable natural creation. It is prodigious to have conceived and executed that first scene in heaven, the walk of the angels, that celestial strut; to have understood Gabriel and known what his mysterious horn looks like; to have known that the everlasting banquet is a fish fry (Heine's intuition of the Talmudic menu was leviathan cooked with garlic) ; to have summed the Apocalypse into that magnificent line, "Gangway for the Lord!"

In the role of the Ancient of Days Himself are both the height of the peril and the apex of the achievement. How does Mr. Connelly know so utterly that the withdrawn shape of their anthropomorphism was just this subtle balance of attributes: an octoroon, not a full-blooded Negro, with a frock coat, an office? By what working of infallible intuition do we know without the possibility of doubt that he is right?

The mere artistic difficulties even when this feat of creation is accomplished are extraordinary. This race, whose adventure in history will perhaps never be paralleled until the human race is invaded and kidnapped by filibusters from another planet, was the most peaceful, amiable peasants in Africa, probably, for the most part, the same Mandingoes whose bowls of milk kept Mungo Park alive. They were snatched suddenly from an environment with which they had made their peace for centuries, brought across an ocean whose existence they had never imagined, taken in chains of a metal they had hardly seen before, and set down to work out their lives tilling new plants in a new land. They left behind them their very gods, their language, their songs, and were given as the sole consolation to replace them this intricate, infinitely complicated story of the Bible—not even in such simplified form as the older churches have brought it to, but the huge amorphous mass, riddled with all the subtly limited rationalisms which all the Protestant-isms have put into it.

And this Book they made their own. They digested it, as if cows might take to a ration of meat and alcohol, as if chickens succeeded in living on the tops of trees. It became a part of them. Strangest of all, the changes it underwent under their spiritual chemistry (as this play most fully reveals) are close to the deepest spirit of the original. The Negro version of heaven is closer to that of the simplest white believer there has ever been, the peasant of the middle ages, down to its last anachronism, than any imitation or anything but a spiritual blood relationship could account for.

This Negro version, then, now set out is also the purest form of Fundamentalism. How much better Mr. Connelly explains what Bryan could never convey, the touching poetry, the ingenuous conjuring away of logical difficulties, the secret charm, let us say, of the Fundamentalist vision of the universe! Men may fight for their religion with arguments on their lips, but in their hearts the hidden motive is always the tinseled candles they saw on the altar when they were children, the light stained glass throws on Sunday mornings, the frock coat and white tie and the old benevolent face they once attributed to God. So Mr. Connelly—what is art but supernatural?—has here explained not only the Negro heart but the kernel of the Fundamentalist position, their vision of the universe. This, O Mencken, is what the Bible belt is trying to say; however unpleasantly they fight, they are defending a Christmas tree.

My last fear was that he would trip up in the end. For the Negro universe is not only child. In the spirituals there is a piercing sweetness which the Old Testament only partly accounts for. In his last act, the best of them all, as it should be in any play, he unerringly eludes all difficulties of taste, all perils of overbalance, and gives us the true, excellent expression of how the very inner room of this suffering people's heart is furnished; with what ultimate hopes, based on what curious theology—Arian, of course, even more than "Paradise Lost"; and Arianism is to Christian theology what common sense is to metaphysics.

This play should finally come triumphant into repertoire; it is made to outlast. I would place it (with a few technical alterations) beside Uncle Remus, and if you knew what I think about Uncle Remus you would think I was exaggerating. I have laid most of the emphasis upon one special side of its charm and importance. Simply as a work of art it is unmistakably genuine; and its author, through it, is received into the best company of the world, that of real artists, which also is in a way celestial, outside which mere talent, brains and cleverness will ever weep, excluded.

✦ 43 ✦

So Passes—

WASHINGTON, March 4.—The Inaugural Procession, which I have tried to witness in the middle of one of the largest and most patient crowds

I have ever seen, has a probably incurable and essential dramatic weakness. I should say that at the beginning its protocol was arranged without the smallest intention of spectacle or forethought of our modern masses.

The kernel is an intimate, dignified affair, half bucolic, half masonic perhaps, strictly among the clubs of illustrious friends who defeated England. Very likely they anticipated with pleasure that the rural community of Washington would put up flags at the bottom of their gardens and run out to raise a friendly cheer as the incoming and outgoing Presidents drove leisurely to and from the induction in the Capitol to their lunches and speeches in the White House. The rest—the interminable vertebral afternoon procession—is accretion, drawn, one imagines, from the only native and traditional ritual of America—the circus.

In consequence, an affair which has the greatest possibilities of the sublime and the pathetic is as disjointed and distended as a Chinese play. Such crucial state functions should be, and are, strangely enough, in all monarchical countries, the highest luxury of the masses; the peak benefits of life in society, in which the meanest classes have the most generous share.

This parade contains, in the nature of things, a combination of two high interests: a funeral and a coronation, the meeting and parting of incoming and outgoing rulers. The first I saw, and almost alone, at about eleven o'clock this morning. Only a narrow and tattered fringe of spectators lined the route so early. The great, phlegmatic row of Ionic pillars of the

Treasury stood out of a wilderness of seats which had its nakedness of timbering and sheeting concealed and deserted.

The dark macadam of the street was dry as yet. The rain came later. Quite suddenly we unsuspecting early comers heard a cheer—a thin-bodied cheer—and a great clatter which made us crane and attend. A regiment of cavalry, picked cavalry, with drawn swords, but not even a trumpet to accompany them as they loped past; row after row of brown sandstone men, intent, untheatrical as the army of Cromwell.

And then behind them, a huge silent car with the two Presidents. Both were looking straight ahead: Mr. Coolidge was making some conventional conversation without turning his head. Mr. Hoover, strained, dumb, gave him back not even monosyllables.

The car went slowly enough for us to watch their faces. The man who now departs into that peculiar oblivion that democracies reserve for their discarded servants, the corner of the attic where Al Smith and so many others already lie dusty, has gained a sharp distinction in his face which no early picture shows, heightened by the rich, soft black of the collar of his coat. He was growing into a great man fast when his term expired; I think to look at him he knows it on this last ride down the Avenue.

The man beside him at this supreme moment of his destiny had a heavy, almost ill-tempered intensity, as if he were waiting for something or trying to find something that exasperated him by its delay. I have seen enough of great men and great occasions to know surely what that look means. The machine will not work, the trigger is jammed, the crown of everything, the thrill, holds off. Mr. Hoover was feeling nothing; the cup of his life's quest at his lips was full of tasteless water. He heard the cheers, he could not listen to them. His brain was telling him he was President at last; his senses made no meaning in the words.

So they passed, the one on his road to the cold abdication the law imposes, the other to a glory his power of enjoyment was not equal to feeling. Neither of them took the slightest notice of our feeble chorus immersed in their own destinies.

Then the monstrous, the insensitive wait, which the bent old machinery of the ritual imposes on the crowd. For three hours and more nothing but a street cleaner's truck and empty street cars passed us. Slowly the bordering stream thickened. Minute after minute new hundreds hurried up, jostled a little, took their seats or their stand, and looked expectantly at the same sights: the dull Ionic pillars; a far off airplane hovering like a dragon fly in the smoky clouds, awaiting the dire moment with its eternal point as sharp as a tenpenny nail.

The rain began to come thicker; away to the left the people in the best seats began to put up their umbrellas to keep off the drip from the leafless planetrees. Gradually the slope became colored with these umbrellas, the blurred purples and violets of a moth's wing.

The rain and the packing increased. The blue surface of the street changed under the myriad winking

188

drops into a dark brown. Vendors came past with queer things, tawdry medals; strangest of all, dolls' heads on sticks, with long tresses of hair, like cannibal mementoes. Every one was wearing a button or a badge —thick-limbed, smiling country people, impressed with the subconscious realization that they belonged to an innumerable horde, and here represented it.

Gradually we began to steam. Women crossed caps for themselves out of their newspapers and put them on to save their hats. A smell of damp paper, damp mackintoshes, damp fur came up; and still the back rows tightened on us.

At last the President has finished his lunch, that interminable, inhumane, uncomprehending meal that would make a revolution at any European coronation if the mob had to wait for it. So far there has not been a single note of music. I know that will come later, and plenty. Accompanied only by the sound of the horses' hoofs of his guard, the new President returns. The old has gone—just as inevitably, completely as if he were dead. Mrs. Hoover sits beside her husband now in the open car in the rain—radiant, enthusiastic, as charming and excited as a May Queen. Behind them, in the next car, waving his tall hat with exaggerated gestures of an almost indiscreet delight, the Vice President, Mr. Curtis.

But the great man himself, still unthrilled, still in a rigid spasm of incomprehension, hat off, sodden and dripping with the rain, bows and smiles mechanically, jerkily, almost ragingly in a vast hurricane of applause.

Sic transit.
They settled for another hour's wait.

✦ 44 ✦

About "The Front Page"

THE theatre is the first omen of magnificence of the things happening to America; the first authentic proof that humanity's depleted stock of things that make life worth living is being enriched with another, new civilization. Therefore the interest, the news, of a play like "The Front Page" spills over the first-night or even the second-night critiques; it is worth not only a six months' belated column but a whole chapter in a history, which I hardly doubt it will one day have.

Two obstacles may have fogged this, at any rate, in the minds of most people I have discussed it with. The one is that inveterate old misunderstanding, the moral point of view: there is an enormous number of people, not necessarily uneducated or pious, who think that the proper use of swearing and slang is the indivisible privilege of Shakespeare. I heard this in its purest form from a drunken poet in a speakeasy. The second —at the stage only of a vague doubt in my mind—is the production; the plain fact is that the play reads even better than it is acted. The Grand Guignolism of the first act, which misadjusts the mind to what is go-

190

About "The Front Page"

ing to be a heroic farce, the factitious speed that drops a third of the sense and a quarter of the dialogue en route, and jumps the points, and overruns the stations, certainly does not improve the play: which is the only ideal of production.

The most amazing result of these or any other astigmatisms is that some poor people have thought they saw an attack on newspaper men. So in that somewhat similar though inferior play, "The Playboy of the Western World," which was the most outrageous flattery of the Irish people, the mob missed the point and rioted. The real parallel to this "Front Page" is "Cyrano de Bergerac"; the only serious difference, leaving out the trivial difference of Rostand's verse form and Hecht and MacArthur's prose, is that the one flattered a dull and mediocre present through the mode of the past, and the others address to the future their wildly enthusiastic picture of the present.

The reporters of Chicago have been put above the cadets of Gascoigne. They have been paladinized, apotheosized near to losing their resemblance to men; their life turned into an epic of adventure, death and battle that would have made Ned Buntline burn his dummy of Buffalo Bill in despair.

I will not trouble to remind you that these demigods do everything romantic, work and gamble all night for nothing, hold mighty villains like the Sheriff and the Mayor by the tails as if they were rats—I have actually heard an intelligent man say that this was blackmail!—and toss them into the garbage can, disdaining to kill them. One of them, Murphy, who after playing for the sympathy of every boy-hearted man in the world by holding off a shrewish alimonist at the cost of the best hand he ever held, in that opening poker game, kicks a desperate gunman in the rear and makes him cry. . . . Stop here, please, and see the unconcealed animus behind that kick; the ruthless partisanship with which Hecht and MacArthur ridicule the claim of mere racketeers to be romantic. Diamond Louie is the real butt of the play; he gets the roughest words, all the physical violence, and stands the big laugh when he brings in his rescue party of one small boy in short pants, a sailor, and a seedy old man of the Trader Horn type to abduct the mahogany desk and its terrific contents from the press room of the Criminal Courts.

Now, the climax of this superb hero worshipping is in the characters of Hildy Johnson and Walter Burns, the demigod reporter and the demigod executive editor. Such is the impetus of the authors' enthusiasm that they must have that unheard-of luxury—two heroes; such their natural genius that each hero subsists intact and heightens the effect of the other. One gives up his girl for a story; the girl, he says broken-heartedly, "has brains, looks, spirit, everything." The other, beside him, is ready and apparently able to burn up the heavens and earth, at least the Central Criminal Courts, to hit the front page.

Somehow, here we mount out of reach of any class of men, even newspaper men, and a national ideal, that frenzied game of work, which Europe has mistaken for materialism, is unrolled like a banner and put into their glorious hands. The unfolding of the events that choke from the escape of Earl Williams from the death chamber and lead up to his capture by the heroes is the biggest and most exciting presentation of men at grips with their job I have ever seen. It is more exciting than a cavalry charge, more breathless than breaking the automobile speed record on the sands, more dramatic than a council of war of an empire in the last ditch.

In such moments of million voltage tension, which only the pure dramatic genius, and only with inspired technique, is able to attain, a vision of reality is always near. We begin to see things, like the witches at the high crisis of their Sabbath. Without the shadow of a written role or the least phrase of a stage direction a great, shaggy phantom begins to emerge from hallucination and take shape through the scene: the ultimately unknowable monster, the sphinx whom every living being in social life must strive to unriddle and love, the public—the public, to whom Hecht and MacArthur have victoriously consecrated the newspaper man priest and champion, the super-villain and super-hero of the play, who condemns and pardons, weeps and gloats, like a god over the spectacle of its own terrors and sorrows. And by setting an almost limitless price on its servants and their efforts they set up in the only possible way the worth of the mob itself.

How far this is, like all the best fruit of genius, come about unconsciously, is an interminable question to debate. There is a good deal of the unconscious and the naif about Hecht and MacArthur: their artistic

certificate. As they naïvely say of one of their characters, the whole play is "full of strange oaths and a
touch of childhood." They say when the great Walter
Burns enters, "That licensed eavesdropper, trouble
maker, bombinator and town snitch misnamed the
press," which is better than Trader Horn ever said on
the subject. It may or may not be the same crowing
affection that brings on Hildy's blasphemy on his
chief. But whether they wanted to or not, who cares?
They have raised the common reporter, the news man,
to a fiery beacon of the imagination, as the last and
most magnetic of adventurers. There is probably more
truth in it than in most heroic legends.

✦ 45 ✦

"Berkeley Square"

JOHN BALDERSTON'S play, "Berkeley
Square," deserves something more than technical
criticism. I noticed and admired particularly, by the
way, the singularly clear and easy explanation of the
abstract scientific hypothesis that he puts into the
mouth of his hero at the beginning. I had often puzzled how one of the most difficult concepts of modern
thought on time and space, on which I knew the
play was based, could be given to the resolutely
unmathematical-minded audience of a theatre. No one
who goes need fear that it will lack that plausibility,

194

issued like a ticket by science, without which it is unusual nowadays to dare to dream.

But it is the scope of the emotional research, even more than such other excellencies, that most pleasantly interests me.

In short, there are two main directions in the play: the "sense of the past," and the theme of hopeless love. The young American, Peter Standish, loses his girl in the past, in a night-fog worse than death. You know the story, how the rather shallow, cold and thin aesthete, by brooding in the old house on the portrait of one of his ancestors who resembled him, flies or falls or dreams himself backward in time to the late middle-age of the eighteenth century, and there, for a day or two, relives and revolves, and unalterably loses his phantasmal heroine.

Perhaps the essence of this situation is in all love. It may even be that it is the shadow of an inevitable end, thrown backward, that is the secret of the unearthliness, the undertone of noble melancholy in such experience, which all the poets have tried to express and in which Shakespeare succeeded. I do not exclusively mean the strange thought that Hardy set in his poem of the woman who was jealous of an old photograph of herself that her lover cherished, and so destroyed it; that the most constant love, like Standish's, is the cult of a fragment, broken out of the perfumed past. I mean that in the highest and most philosophic and most poetical passion, like the great bourdon in the chimes of Orleans, may have to lie the foreknowledge of death.

Camera Obscura

If you had known
When listening with her to the far-down moan
Of the white-selvaged and empurpled sea . . .
You would lay roses
Fifty years thence on her monument that discloses
Its graying shape upon the luxuriant green . . .

Or, at any rate, so the old experts in the disappearing art of life all say.

If this be so, then Mr. Balderston has set out for us a scene of true love in the old tradition, now I suppose, as unused as the old Provençal way of making thin glass out of the ashes of hedge-canes, or any other picturesque secret the new ways have put out of use. To this he has added, I hardly think involuntarily, a sub-acid raillery at modernity in the character of his hero. For this hero is modern even to his faults, which are not so much of the heart—though his behavior to his flesh and blood world is sheer muflerie, as the French call social unimagination—but also of the wits. How deliciously sideways does our author avenge his own romanticism on the modern young man by putting him face to face for counted moments with the pale phantasmal thing he loves, which, once gone, he will never find again. He knows he will waste all the billions of years in eternity talking of the plumbing and lighting of modern New York, of aeroplanes, of Ford cars, of the stagy side of the late war, of tanks and of gas masks. And, mark you, he will talk of these things in the absurd proprietorial tone we all use about the mechanical inventions of our days, as if it were we individually who made them.

Peter Standish, whirled into this strange and beautiful adventure, never ceases to be one of us. He flounders in it at every turn. He is almost as inwardly ill at ease as the terrible Yankee at the Court of King Arthur. Once the mere sightseeing has passed, once he has seen the sedan chairs pass in the tranquil streets, talked with the august dead and heard them talk, exhausted the possibilities of investment in real old masters at a hundred guineas each, and used on them, as the other did on the seigneurs of the Round Table, his lasso and revolver, the aphorisms of Wilde, the longing for our own age, for its baths and cigarettes, comes back on him.

Excellent, smooth satire. I suppose we are like that; that in a tour of eternity down the spinning years to the dawn of life we should be obsessed all the way by the progressive lack of hygiene. People come back from Japan every year who have noted only that the natives are dirty and eat a lot of rice.

Nevertheless, it is this sly notation of Standish's spiritual vulgarity that makes him real and dramatic. The stretched credibility is ribbed and strengthened by the solid flesh and blood of the hero's personality. A hero who was at the height of the opportunity, who would not find bows and hand-kisses extraordinary, who could think deeply enough to offset the strangling and burning of a wife who poisoned her husband— there is some historical mistake about her being a witch, if the time is 1780—against the fate of Mrs. Snyder, and talk about neither, would perhaps be more romantic but would risk floating with the play into the unbreathable air of pure fantasy. As it is, Standish is real. The play, too ; so much so that not once but many times, helpless in the power of author and actors, I, who feel with difficulty the illusion of the theatre, had the authentic shudder of the supernatural, the readjustment to the deeper reality of the mystery of life, death and love that, however the street roars and burns in our days, still and forever surrounds us.

✦ 46 ✦

Whalen's Education

IT is rare that so simple a personality as that of Whalen becomes a capital interest to a vast community. Everything he does, every step in his reeducation by the City of New York, which is perhaps the deepest aspect of his career in office, goes to confirm the first estimate I made of him when he took office. That is, here is an honest, brave, quite unsophisticated man, with one of the finest and most complete sets of undeveloped ideas on government, law, social ideals, who has ever emerged into a position of great public trust. He had (for this is by no means an obstinate character) a sort of political virginity. No doubt many other officials, maybe in secret, are

pretty much in agreement with him in the main part
of his errors. But all of them that I can suspect of
this have the cunning to hide it, with a deft and appro-
priate use of cant. There is nothing canting about
Mr. Whalen, which makes him a priceless specimen
for the studies of political philosophers.

There are many angles in him that catch the light
sufficiently well to serve as entrance to such a study.
I choose his extraordinary faith in common sense or (it
amounts to the same thing) his perfect ignorance of
political tradition as anything else but vaguely
remembered words and phrases. He started his
job absolutely fresh, tackling every problem as it
arose with the sole assistance of his own spontaneous
idea.

You may remember, for example, that almost the
first thing that confronted him was the gang problem.
He was the man who was going to clean up the Roth-
stein case. The city was alarmed at the confusing
nightmare the facts and the art of reporting had combined to conjure up of an "empire of the underworld,"
"unpunished crime stalking brazenly through the
streets," &c.

And so Mr. Whalen found at once a simple way of
stopping it. The law's delay had been accused as one
of the chief factors in the situation; Mr. Whalen announced a simple, common sense, business way of clear-
ing this out of the way. You will remember what it
was. The police were instructed to use their night-
sticks in immediate, exemplary punishment of any
"criminal characters" they came across, trying, con-

demning and punishing them without the idiotic for-
malities of trial, without the risk of lawyers tangling
up the case, without the possibility of the punctilious
formalizing of any old Judges being given a chance to
confuse and delay things. Mr. Whalen took no notice
of the theoretical implications of such a clean-cut
plan, of course. The whole force of his character is
that such implications never spontaneously occur to
him.

Yet such implications not only existed but were
grave and real enough to raise a long howl of protest
and anguish among the rest of the body of the citizens.
Habeas corpus, jury trial, laws, rights of accused per-
sons . . . things that centuries of martyrdom, millions of martyrs, had won, it appears, still have some
validity and value. Mr. Whalen's extemporaneous
version of a higher lynch law to supersede all these
old things was heartily refused, and he was asked to
think again.

This he did with the utmost good humor, and with,
as it were, a candid look of surprise which is the most
attractive feature of a very sympathetic soul. He had
not thought of that. He was willing to learn. For, remember, Mr. Whalen is a good pupil. Once a thing
is explained to him, and he sees the sense of it, he is
quite ready to adopt it. Without this faculty his career
in power could not be described as what I call "a
political education." Nor perhaps would it have been
so long.

So here was his first lesson: that laws and legality

are not just nonsense, not invented by some grafters at Runnymede in favor of the criminal classes, but the sure bulwark of the law-abiding.

The rest of the curriculum must be summed up quickly, so that I can come to the page in his lesson-book which lies open before him to-day. From settling the whole Prohibition problem by the quick method of closing "every speakeasy in New York" he came to be educated in those deep matters of public opinion, natural moral resilience, economic compulsion, so that now he only fights with speakeasies "which are a breeding ground of criminals and which sell poison booze." A little while ago he started on the problem of the flighty girl, immoral dancing places—solved in five minutes this interestingly tangled part of the ancient vast social conundrum of prostitution—and probably by now is finding, with the intellectual delight of a good student, that that, too, has a history, that that, too, has been tried before.

But now the problem of the Reds. Here, too, is an ancient problem, an infinitely, intricately insoluble tangle. Mr. Whalen, as always, finds it shockingly easy at first. Take his enthusiastic announcement that he "sent members of the police force into the Communist demonstration and that they carried placards demanding the overthrow of the Government and that they made as much noise as genuine Reds."

Alas, Mr. Whalen, this, too, is not new, and this, too, has a history of failure. They have even in the long and disastrous use of this "common-sense device" put a dirty name on it. It is what is called the system of the "agent provocateur."

The Czar's Government was expert at it. Napoleon III of France tried it so hard and skilfully that M. Claude, his Chief of Police, once counted 60 per cent. of a Red council meeting who were known to him as detectives. Yet it did not work, perhaps never has worked, perhaps always makes matters worse. Is it not confusing to a common-sense man to find all these problems so very old, so very complicated?

But if a Police Commissioner is too busy to look at the acres of shelves of historical literature in the matter, accounts of how many times it has been tried before, and how many times it has failed, there is a gorgeous novel by Joseph Conrad called "The Secret Agent" in which are all the essentials.

Mr. Whalen should read that. But for the rest of his scheme for abolishing political sin, the communication of names of members of the Communist Party to their employers for dismissal—for that, to learn how it has been tried on the grandest scale over and over again in the history of the world, there is nothing to be done but to read the whole history of the persecution of ideas. This "victimization" has never worked. I think I know underlying all reasons why it has not worked, though it looks so enticing, is, above all, that justice must never use injustice in its fight on injustice —for fear of making it just. How complicated! But Mr. Whalen is now tackling, as it were, the college grade in his education by the facts of life, and the City of New York and he must expect that.

The Last Bow

THE return of Sherlock Holmes and the last bow of William Gillette made together at the New Amsterdam a singularly fascinating event. It had a quite suitable setting.

The profuse art nouveau of the decoration is old enough now to be interesting. I fancy this style, which once looked as if eternity itself could not digest it, will seem mighty poetical and perfumed and touching in a mere century or so. Fine specimens will certainly be rare, for in the post-war period it has been more relentlessly proscribed and wantonly destroyed than the bison, or Gothic in the days of Queen Anne.

They may some day envy us who saw the New Amsterdam in perfect condition and completeness: the lilies growing out of its panels, stage boxes like tiers of fungus on a tree stump, every door jamb in flower and fruit.

At the top, hanging from the ceiling are some mysterious things, like parrots' or macaws' cages, covered up for the night with green baize dustbags.

William Gillette conceals his age with all his masterly make-up technique. It is as it should be: that we should not see him with gray hair, or with face lines.

He has not come back to play for our sympathy but admiration. This, every one in the house gives him whenever he allows it. The scene endings let loose full, crackling electric storms of hand-clapping that last for five minutes at a time. When he comes before the curtain and makes a queer inhibited speech to us, there is an uproar of joy.

But still this long, straight man, as light as a ghost, as brittle, it seems to me whenever he enters, as a tall glass vase, never shocks us by pretending to be young. There is absolutely no spot of pathos in him, or the play. He and it belong to the past—that is, to a present that is grown illustrious.

The play itself was clearly composed from the first and last stories of the original series. Half of it is "A Scandal in Bohemia," from the "Adventures," and half "The Final Problem," from the "Memoirs." One is allowed to be pedantic only in such matters. The girl then comes from the first story, before Doyle has quite finished the outline of his character, and Professor Moriarty, arch-villain, from the last.

The audience's semi-comical disappointment at the ending, at Holmes in the arms of a little girl, preparing for holy matrimony, is therefore only three-quarters the fault of the author. Is it not written that "there was a woman. In his eyes she eclipses and predominates the whole of her sex"? See the very first line of the very first page of the "Adventures." But it was truly near sacrilege to forget what canonically follows: "All emotions, and that one particularly, were abhorrent to his cold, precise but admirably balanced mind."

I do not care much that the first lovers of the detective themselves tolerated and even approved Mr.

The Last Bow

Gillette's daring. Sherlock Holmes was not a mortal man to marry a pretty client like a mere Arsène Lupin.

I have long meditated the basic mystery of Holmes. Not his literary standing; as to that, he is quite good writing, obviously of the same school as Robert Louis Stevenson, that also produced, if you remember, its most brilliant alumnus, Rudyard Kipling. I go as far in this temperate judgment as to include "The Return" and passages at any rate of "His Last Bow," rejecting as apocalyptic, and probably by a feigned hand—on internal evidence, a Chicago cub reporter's —the perfectly terrible Case Book, with its weak rubbish of the devil's foot, Sussex vampire and all the rest, which do not merit that any one should recall even their names.

But many depths beneath this, and many miles within, Sherlock Holmes is not to submit to any simply literary court. His narrative is Stevenson, his origin Poe. But he himself is something more than a book, as are Pickwick, Uncle Toby, the Caliph Vathek, Count Fosco, Heathcliff, and many scores more, happily, of the creations of English genius. He is an extra-human personality, a living individual added outside the flesh to the sum of men on the earth.

Doyle himself came upon creation almost suddenly, as accidents occur. I related his ever so slight stumble at the beginning, where he toyed with the idea of a Holmes in love—at once to reject it. The spirit of a town and time cannot be given in marriage.

Holmes is the fog in that crying old street, Baker Street, the glow of sea coal in the grates, where the

English servant brings in to you tea and muffins, and snug napkins of odorous toast. He is especially the spirit that your curiosity calls up every time you visit this city, which is richer in phantoms of a sort than Peking or Angkor, the mystery of the house opposite, of the grubby little shop around the corner you noticed and wondered about, of the old, old lady, half perceived in her shining brougham, who passes through empty Eaton Square every Wednesday afternoon. Sherlock is he who answers when you ask the air, Who lives there, I wonder? What is the story behind that drawn blind in London? So he, almost better than any other, will tell you that city which is an ocean in time as well as space removed from you; and William Gillette is his guaranteed medium.

Therefore the right request to make of Gillette (before you are too late) is not to give you only a thriller which is mechanically perfect, comparing with our thrillers like that of a music box to a gramophone; incidents so neatly turned that the whole audience gives them without prompting the exactly right response of contented laughter.

All of this he does, notoriously. But from him you may expect something much too subtle to be advertised. Cabs slurring through mud, sounds and sights and presences of the old nineties in Baker Street, that time and that place which above all thought itself final, and that nothing different was ever going to happen again.

Did you ever read the great bed table classic, the "Diary of a Nobody"? If it is among your books, read it when you come back from seeing Gillette. Between them will infallibly arise, gently, around you as you fall asleep, feelings and thoughts about life, yourself, everything that matters, the satisfying balance between the transience and the permanence of all things, that will give you good dreams better than even the mandragora-syrup prescription of Othello.

✦ 48 ✦

Carnera

THE coming of Primo Carnera is a major event to I do not care to guess how many millions of men of all nationalities to-day. At Detroit, or behind the Chicago stockyards, in the ruined collier villages of the north of England, on the quai-sides of Venice, New York, and for all I know Shanghai, they are discussing it over their lunch pails at this very moment.

Sport is the chief share they have to-day in the drama of life. Even in France and Spain it has superseded politics as the predominant masculine interest. Politicians are in despair about it. And boxing is the innermost shrine of the cult—alas, too often empty. For this universal "sporting public," which numerically is almost synonymous with the whole of the modern industrial and business world, is strictly dependent on the caprice of nature. The crops depend on the fantasy of the seasons, in the last resort. The boxing cult depends on the still less predictable will of nature to produce a rare type of man. For your great prizefighter must not only have the strength, the skill, the courage. He has to have a specially dramatic or heroic personality, which experience has demonstrated is almost as rare as a poet, much less common than great captains of industry or statesmen. The demi-gods of the ring have to have as many points, as seldom found together, as an avatar of Vishnu. We have to wait till nature is in a mood for artistic production.

The heavyweight contender—that is the most convenient name for them—must be an embodiment of the strange and unusual, yet elemental, qualities, so that grown men of imagination may adopt him, and play with him. He must be material for folk lore, like Dempsey, Carpentier, Tunney, Johnson, Jeffries—a gorilla man, or a dude, or a terror, or a romance. Just a first class pugilist is not much use to the faithful.

Once found, these intangible, artistic qualities must be developed and heightened, as a diamond is set and polished, by the specialists, who take him in hand, managers and press agents. They have a curious and naïve technique. Tex Rickard was an adept at it, for clarifying and simplifying the natural image of the man. Sometimes, rarely, they emphasize an heroic quality. That worked well with Tunney. Better and easier, they exaggerate the monstrous they find in him. They make a tiger out of the amiable Dempsey, a strangler out of another, a black terror out of the blithe and irresponsible Jack Johnson. Sometimes the

Carnera

picture of a mere coward will do for these bards; anything that flares up emotions of hate, admiration or wonder. So Carnera has to be at all costs the giant.

Carnera in cold fact is not pathologically a giant. He is not a gland freak, that is, a pituitary monster (though perhaps slightly acrocephalic), but simply a very big, strong fellow. By the dressing-room scales, he has shrunk from the some 7 feet his poetical manipulators sang to merely 6 feet 6½.

And yet, artistically, they are right. As Carnera climbs into the ring, there is certainly something shockingly abnormal about him. Whatever his measurements, this bulk has a little air of nightmare. The eye fixes aghast on a horrible, bright green cloth cap, a bawdy color like cheap green baize, a jutting, canaille peak. I admire the artist who had him wear that cap; it is the toughest cap in the world, and more frightening than the hood of a ghost.

When he has taken it off and the matched dressing gown, you see that his barrel body, red and chapped, is stuck into a pair of gaudy silk drawers, with a wild boar in a lozenge on them in staring red and green. There is a grotesque femininity about this enormous, badly cut garment which escapes none of the hearty jokes of the crowd. Big Boy Peterson, the weakly good-natured looking human being in the opposite corner, licks his lips and turns his eyes to the ground.

The situation then is: every one wants eagerly Carnera to prove himself really what he looks like. His managers, because of the millions that they will share. His nation and Europe generally, for a sort of patriotism; and the whole world public, indeed, thirsty for drama. But there are the rules of reality in the matter. We are not children but men; we want to believe. But he must help our disbelief. Of course he will win this fight. But he must win it convincingly. Above all, is he fast? Otherwise, he is not theatre, but merely circus.

The realization of this vital requirement is the rather amusing secret of his antics. After each blow, or rather, as they looked to me, pushes with a tear in them, as a bear would give, he executes a queer shuffling break down. He has only to give three blows. He executes Big Boy rather than fights him. It lasts only a minute.

The high priests are satisfied with the omens. The dressing room is packed. I think this inner world of sports, with its own learning, its own quiet and polite etiquette, its respectable and human ethical code, is very remarkable and enjoyable. Ned Brown, Ed Van Every (the author of the excellent "Muldoon"), were there, and Ed Sullivan; scores more—a picked company.

I now saw and spoke to the giant face to face. His face especially is remarkable. An ecstatic touching smile; he is a Venetian pile driver, and now in reach of incredible riches. The thoughts of feasts, women, clothes, are dancing in his head. His teeth are all shown, long and yellow like a horse's, with receding gums and dark at their base. There is only an inch between his forehead and his eyes, and there is a red mark chafed on the bridge of his formless nose. The inordinate length of his face, the strange, unspeculative look in his stare, his great sensuous lips, would be familiar in decadent Rome; the Rome of Nero and Faustina. He is a gladiator such as they used to carve on the prow of their pleasure galleys in the days of Petronius.

It is wrong to say he has a beautiful or even noble body. It is red and hairless. His muscles are the plebeian masses that merge roundly into each other, with the look of fatness; the muscles of a blacksmith or stevedore, not the aristocratic flesh pure sport creates. His skin, too, is muddy. There was a large angry-red pimple on his shoulder, and his huge feet are lamentable; bunioned, jointed, the feet of a poor waiter. On his left calf there are knotted veins and the scars of boils or festered bruises.

As they photographed him I saw his manager beside him bend his knees, so that Carnera would look even taller.

"Journey's End"

"JOURNEY'S END" turned out to be gold: the best film of the War. Reversing the natural law of cinematic gravitation that seems to work everywhere else, it actually increased in dramatic interest and tension, like a good play. When Stanhope stumbles at last up the steps of the dugout to find what has had a rendezvous with him for three hellish years, there comes a gradual darkness. For whole minutes, measured by the heart, not the watch, the audience watched all lights but one, the candle in the bully-tin, fade; and at last that went out, and unable to move or blink, forgetting that we were merely looking at an unlighted screen, we sat and peered in silence into primeval night, the end to which only high and true tragedy can lead us securely.

Several things make this quite naïve tragedy of the English a little local. I have actually come across a critic, a friendly one too, who did not understand that the drunkenness of Stanhope is the measure of his superhuman courage. The mere mention of "three years," his front line service, did not convey quite enough explanation, apparently. Well, if you look at the boy Raleigh, and realize that what happened to him was merely the horrors of one day, you may get the three-yearer Stanhope in scale. But Stanhope, company officer, had a dreadful weight to carry, above all the burden of the rest. He alone could have got out of it, at any rate for a time. His exact position is, therefore, that having reached, long ago, the limits of merely human endurance, not even backed by any absolute necessity to continue, he uses the bottle for the last mile. He knows that for this aid he has to pay the last hope, the very last, of any happiness in life should he by any miracle escape. For whenever the war should end, it would find him a hopeless drunkard, a broken man.

"Journey's End"

And then there is the so-curious authentic English "vital mannerism." That is in the first place, even here on the threshold of eternal night, they are all a little snobbish. To an English ear minute tonal varieties of pronunciation convey all the time that Stanhope, Trotter and all the rest are still—how shall I put it?—socially conscious. It is one of the grand prepossessions of the race. The English can convey more in an intonation than the Chinese; from the mere pitch of their voices, as well as from their choice of words, any English audience could repeat, what the actors certainly meant to convey, the whole background, the style of school, the houses their characters were likely to live in; and many other more difficult spiritual things. These are not just any Englishmen. They are subspecies of an involved social subspecies.

Connected with this is the small scale some foreigners think they find in their number of emotions. They behave astonishingly different from all other soldiers under a like stress—if you like, you may say that compared with the Germans, revealed by Remarque and Wasserman, or the Frenchmen of Barbusse, they are mere schoolboys. To some this may diminish the grandeur of their tragedy, this specific unripeness, unadultness of intellectual range, which the author superbly sums up in his famous choice of Alice as a last reading. To me it heightens the tragedy: that they are all so innocent.

Yet, with this at any rate mental innocence, nevertheless Stanhope can find and use in extremity, when he has to argue the poor devil who is frightened into dying, the most subtle dialectic of heroism.

There is the whole wisdom of the soldier, which is a deep part of the whole body of wisdom, in his argument: "Why commit suicide? Let the enemy do it for you."

And now for the very last consideration. All nations drawn into this last "great battle in the west" seem, looking back, to have prepared the souls of their young men for it through the whole of their histories. Each national culture had its own style of doing this. The English preparation, it seems to me, was poetical. There is an obscure presentiment in all their poets from Shelley, perhaps from Shakespeare, to Browning, and even Kipling. They were all steeped to an incredible degree in poetry, this generation that stumbles up the stairs with Stanhope into eternal loss; more than you would believe actually died with lines of poetry on their lips; and a poetical attitude to life and death can easily be mistaken unwarily for a young immature one.

So they died, whose irreplaceable loss England will probably feel for as many centuries as the passing of Arthur in that other Western campaign, Stanhope and his crowd, not with philosophical, nor even with entirely patriotic motives in their hearts, but with something I find much finer and more touching. It is in the revelation of this that "Journey's End," both play and now film, is ultimately to be prized.

Over the Air

I EAGERLY accepted the invitation to drop into the dinner of the Economic Club, with the raisins and nuts, because business captains are fascinating and mysterious to me. Here were a thousand head of them, real big game, feeding under natural conditions; and rarest and best occasion of all, at grips with general ideas.

Art, education, civilization itself were on the agenda, for the set toast of the evening was the future of radio.

So far in my rare observations, I have only seen them under unfavorable conditions, either lost in the jungle of political argument, or on the inaccessible peaks of their native technologies, where my untrained eye follows them with strain. To-night I could see them in the open.

I will pass over the Chairman, Gen. James G. Harbord, whose interruptions were without special interest. A good example of the easy, competent wisecracker school of after-dinner rhetoric, which is now standard. There is a lot of rather pessimistic psychology in the thing but it is subtle and dry.

It is notoriously easy to make business men laugh, as soon as there are more than a dozen together; and the General exploited this remorselessly.

Like a good newspaper man I will put the best first.

215

This was David Sarnoff, the brain and will of the Radio Corporation. I had occupied the gaps in the interest of a speech by a Congressman, who preceded him, by private guessing which of the big men at the best three tables Sarnoff would turn out to be. I was wrong. The vulture men, the owners of the imperial noses, the scissors-jawed men all remained seated. The man who got the roar of the well-fed thousand, whose fortunes he had made or increased as he walked to the pulpit was not picturesque, a cylindrical, unimposing man with no more expression than a ship's boiler. He would be hard to caricature. Nevertheless, as he talked, there was a lot to watch, both in his face and in the technique of his mind. One obvious peculiarity was that his cheeks were muscled like Dempsey's arms; you could see them working curiously as he talked.

He never used a pronoun for radio; never once called it "it," always "radio." Just as wellbred children (in my days) were never allowed to speak of their mother as "she." Who is "she"? My grandmother would say sternly, "the cat's aunt?" It was reverent.

Mr. Sarnoff's mental quality is evidently concentration, which is a sort of courage. It is impossible to knock him off the thread; every time the thousand bellowed, he was waiting with the next word, exactly where he left off. I surmise this is the fundamental reason of his success—this logical stubbornness, that conquers the diffusiveness of board meetings, the confusion of corporate wills faced with decisions. How many times must groups of directors, tired and lost in

216

their arguments, have turned with relief to Sarnoff sitting there calmly nursing the essentials.

But this evening this master of the business syllogism, this one-idealled man, has to leave his firm base and adventure himself into regions where every promise is debatable, among mysteries beside which even that of radio is simple. What is humanity going to do with radio? Or rather what is radio going to do with humanity?

A new incalculable has leapt into the equation: one which is no mere physical quantity to be conjured out of the way with cunning mathematics of probabilities, by a living mischievous thing. Mr. Sarnoff is down to tell us not only that in ten years every home in the United States will have telephony and television; he has built a theatre for 120,000,000 people, all seats free. Now what program is he going to give them every night in the year, forever? Whether he likes it or not, he has to think about art and genius.

So far these hard business men have never discovered a region where economic law does not reign. Where Demand does not bring in brother Supply at the double. Every material commodity they require exists in practically illimitable quantity; rubber, copper, the ether itself. But the invisible thing all these are only the vehicle for—Art, Drama, Music—by no means obey the same laws, if any at all. The substance for which all this magical apparatus is only the distributing agency is the product of Genius, and that no system, no need, no discoverable sequence has ever been able to increase, foster or influence into growth in the slightest degree.

What will happen, Mr. Sarnoff, when this universal public has heard the small stock of music that is worth while that you have inherited, until it knows it by heart? What will happen when with the aid of that highly competent educator Damrosch you have given a hundred million people the taste that will not endure mediocrity—and you have nothing new and good to give them? When the televisionists are tired of the rubbish that the first novelty will make palatable— put it at fifty years if you like—where is the Radio Corporation going to find the genius that will make the marvel of inventors, scientists and organizers anything but a tantalizing toy?

To this Sarnoff answered clearly, sensibly and wrongly. He has the same optimism I have remarked in the only other practical men interested in the subject: Bolshevists. M. Tchitcherin told me his views on Genius, the only thing that makes human existence and progress worth while: "It will come all right." Sarnoff thinks it will come. Sarnoff thinks that God will send it in due time. All this education, all these facilities, all this immense reward which we dimly perceive accumulating, this audience of the universe ought to produce an adequate supply of genius.

It will not. If 3,000,000 uneducated Elizabethan Englishmen grow one Shakespeare, how many should the State of New York have? If Athens had 60,000 inhabitants and sixty first class poets, what is the level of creative art in Detroit?

Over the Air

How awful, now just imagine, if this marvelous achievement were only to result in the creation of a vast and perfect instrument that no one could play. If the conquest of the air and space, far beyond the legitimate bounds of the imagination, only resulted as it has hitherto, in Lasky films, in chatter between stockholders and their wives separated by the Atlantic, and in the vast disillusionment of a Nation seated with overwhelming hunger before an empty plate!